Digital Workflow Pocket Primer

Pocket Primer

Pocket Primer

Ric Withers

Portions of this book are adapted from *Digital Workflow*
by Ric Withers and used with permission.

Requests for permission or further information should be addressed to:
Permissions Department
Windsor Professional Information, LLC
11835 Carmel Mountain Road, Suite 1304
San Diego, CA 92128

This and other books in this Pocket Primer series are available at special
quantity discounts for use as premiums and sales promotions, or for use
in corporate training programs. For more information, please contact:
Special Sales
Windsor Professional Information, LLC
11835 Carmel Mountain Road, Suite 1304
San Diego, CA 92128
858-487-2945   Fax: 858-487-3279
e-mail: windsorpub@earthlink.net

Library of Congress Cataloging-in-Publication Data
On file with the Library of Congress
ISBN 1-893190-08-0

Printed in the United States of America
First edition   A B C D E

Credits:
Copy Editor: Phyllis DeBlanche
Production Management: LUX Design, San Diego
Cover Design: Douglas Hyldelund

Foreword

The ultimate and ideal workflow is a totally digital workflow. Unfortunately, in only a few instances is this the case in this industry. Traditional print publishing is plagued by incompatible equipment and disconnected islands of automation. Electronic publishing has created, unintentionally, entirely new forms of digital bottlenecks. Work does not flow in many cases.

The paragraph above contains two key terms: "islands of automation" and "bottleneck." *Islands of automation* refers to those highly automated processes inside the workflow that do not have continuity with the other steps or processes that follow in the workflow. It is like having computer-to-plate technologies and not having reliable digital proofing. The benefits of having a filmless and time-effective platemaking process are diminished by the fact that some customers require a film-based proof. A *bottleneck* is any process or workstation with capacity less than or equal to the demands placed on it. Capacity is the measure of the system output. For example, on a printing press, it is the number of impressions that it can produce in a given time frame, usually an hour.

Every process is composed of many steps. Every step or production operation has a certain capacity. The capacity of each of these operations is not the same. Some stations work faster than others, meaning that at some point some workstations will be idle while others will be overloaded. In the case of islands of automation, we may have very fast, highly automated processes linked with slower processes that will constitute system bottlenecks. The problem with bottlenecks is that they determine the capacity of the entire system. If in my system I have very fast workstations linked to others that are not so fast, the capacity of my system equals the capacity of the slowest workstation, not the fastest.

To be effective, workflows should be entirely automated. In the printing industry, we talk about automation, digital file transfers, etc., but the full benefits of the technology will not be seen if a fully digital workflow is not in place.

I think you will find Ric Withers very helpful in building the workflow you need.

Frank Romano
Series Editor

Introduction

Several years ago I was asked by a quick printer to help with the installation of a polyester computer-to-plate device and a connected color copier. Like many other companies, they were seeking to add direct digital processes in an attempt to expand their services. They already had experience with using high-end desktop publishing software, though mostly for single-color typesetting. We both felt the installation of the new equipment would be relatively straightforward.

As it turned out, the process was anything but easy. Certainly the equipment was installed without problems. But the effects of changing their technology, especially in terms of their platesetting process, had ramifications that extended throughout the rest of the company. The staff needed extensive retraining in how to accept jobs digitally and what was involved in converting previously analog jobs into a digital format. Estimating software needed to be updated. New materials needed to be ordered and inventoried.

As we moved through the process, I began to realize that the success or failure of this new technology hinged on adjusting the business process. Success depended not on the ability of the new equipment to function correctly but on the company's ability to adjust their methods so that the new technology could fit. That relationship between technology and process was workflow.

Later, as I moved back to working with commercial printing, I began paying careful attention to technology problems that would occur in the company. In almost every case, a "technology" problem could only be solved by modifying the business process. The company was much larger and more complex than the quick printer, but the fundamental issue was the same.

The information in this book is designed to represent workflow as a balance between understanding technology and understanding the environment in which that technology functions. As companies seek to change their basic process from working with film to working with digital files—from analog to digital workflow—understanding the implications and effects on the rest of their business process becomes the single most important factor in maintaining, and, it is hoped, building, profitability.

Effective management decisions in today's graphic arts marketplace require an understanding of technology *and* business practices. I hope this book helps you to understand how this relationship functions within your own company under the guise of workflow.

Ric Withers

Contents

Foreword iii

Introduction v

1. The Workflow Focus 1
Workflow Is Not Just Technology 1
Technology—The Inside Push 2
Customer Demands—The Outside Push 6
Return on Investment vs. Remain in Business................................7
The Scientific Approach to Printing..8
Goals of This Book 9

2. Why Digital..11
Monitors, Mice, and Floppies 13
From CEPS to DTP..15
RIPs and PostScript..15
Development of Imagesetters 16
Color and Multiple-Page Imagesetters 17
Computer to Plate (CTP) 18
Digital Printing and Direct to Press..19

3. Digital Workflow—
    Why Now?...21
Advantages of Digital Technology 21
Redefined Roles in a Digital Production Process............................23
Internet Effects 25

Effect on Strategic Planning 25
Film vs. Digital File 26

4. Standards
in the Graphic Arts 29
What Is a Standard? 29
Open vs. Proprietary Systems 30
Types of Standards 31
ISO 32
ANSI 32
CGATS 32
CIE 32
ICC 32
Published Characterizations of Print Processes 33
SWOP 34
SNAP 35
GRACoL 36

5. Workstations
for Workflow 37
Central Processing Unit—CPU 37
Random-Access Memory—RAM 39
Hard Drives—Permanent Storage 40
Removable Media 40
Monitors 41
VRAM and Video Cards 41
Peripherals 42
Operating Systems 43
Macintosh Operating System 43
Windows 3.1/95/98 44
Windows NT 45
UNIX 45
Purchasing Considerations 46

6. Networks—
The Tie That Binds 47
Speed 48
Packets 48

LocalTalk 48
Ethernet 49
TCP/IP 50
Hubs, Bridges, and Routers 50
When To Call an Expert 52

7. Servers...53
What Is a Server?..53
The Client/Server Relationship 54
Macintosh Servers 54
Windows NT 55
UNIX 55
Novell Netware..55
File Servers...56
Print Servers 58
Applications Servers...60
Workflow Servers 60
Server Backup and Maintenance.................................62
Server Security 62

8. Storage...65
Need for Storage...65
Removable Hard Disks and SyQuest...........................67
Magneto Optical Disks..68
Iomega ZIP 68
Iomega JAZ (and the end of SyQuest)........................69
CD-ROM 69
CD-R...70
DAT 70
DVD 71
The Connectivity Nightmare 71
SneakerNet..71
Backup and Archiving...72
Legacy and Obsolescence 74
Internet Effects on Transport Media 75

9. File Formats
    and Digital Art 77

File Type vs. Art Type..77
Native File Formats...79
Text Files..79
Raster and Continuous-Tone Art 80
Resolution 81
Bit Depth 82
Line Art...83
Color Depth 84
File Formats for Raster Images...85
Digital Illustrations and Vector Art......................................86
Using Vector Art 88
File Formats for Vector Art...88
PostScript Files...89
Intermediary Files 90
Adobe PDF 92
TIFF/IT 92
File Formats for Multimedia and On-Line Documents.................93

10. Image Acquisition
and Management...95
Scanner Evolution 97
Defining Scanner Characteristics 98
Photomultiplier Tube Scanners 99
Charge-Coupled Device Scanners 99
Copy-Dot Scanners 100
Fundamentals of Color Reproduction 100
Adjusting Scans for Different Original Types.....................103
Color-Management Software..105
ICC Problems 107
Image Management and OPI...108

11. Proofing
in the Graphic Arts...111
The Proofing Cycle...112
Traditional Proofs 114
Digital Proofs...115
Dye-Sublimation and Thermal Wax Proofers.....................117
Toner Proofers 117

Inkjet Proofers 118
Halftone Digital Proofers 118
Soft Proofing 119
Remote Proofing 120
Special Cases in Proofing 121

12. Raster Image Processor 123
Interpretation 124
Object/Display List 125
Rasterizing and Streaming 128
Spots, Dots, and Pixels 128
Separating the RIPing Process 132
Task Integration in RIPs 133

13. Marking Engines 135
Toner-Based Devices 135
Inkjet Printers 137
Imagesetters 139
Platesetters 141
Polyester and Paper Plates 143
Thermal Imaging Systems 144
Direct Imaging and Digital Presses 147

14. Digital Beyond Prepress 149
Redefining the Document 149
Document Management 151
Job Tickets and Tracking 152
Materials and Labor Tracking 153
Press and Post-Press Control 155

15. Tasks in a Digital
    Production Workflow 157
Creation 159
Preflight 160
Image Capture 160
Page Preparation 161
File Repair 161
Image Swapping 162

Imposition 162
Trapping 163
Proofing 164
Hold for Approval 165
Raster Image Processing 165
Output/Imaging 165
Backup/Archiving 166
Information Systems 166
Create Logic Blocks That Fit Your Structure 167

16. Task Integration
and Location 169
Reorganization and Reengineering 171
Organizing Participants in the Workflow 173
Information Resources 175
Organizing Tasks in the Workflow 178
Measurement and Indicators 182
Allocating Resources To Match Production Flow 183
Correction Cycles 185

17. Automation
in the Workflow 189
Automation in Closed Production Cycles 190
Automation in Open Production Cycles 191
Automating Color 192
Automation in Document Management 195
Scripts 197
Hot Folders 199
Templates 200
Automating Archiving and Backup 201
Automation in Proprietary Workflow Systems 201

18. Workflow
and Process Management 203
Business Environment 204
Changing the Manufacturing Process 206
Key Workflow Indicators 210

19. Identifying
    and Tracking Workflow 213
Workflow Tools 213
How Deep Should You Look? 217
Other Mapping Strategies 219

Conclusion 221

Glossary 225

Index 235

Chapter 1

The Workflow Focus

In the rush of workflow systems and workflow solutions available to the graphic arts industry in the late 1990s, it's easy to see how confusion has overwhelmed those responsible for controlling the work that gets done in a printing shop. Workflow, and particularly digital workflow, has become the most tossed-around term in the industry. It's used to describe everything from new desktop computers to complete systems costing well over a million dollars. Everything, it seems, has somehow become a workflow solution.

Workflow Is Not Just Technology
Imagine the plight of someone who has just purchased some sort of new, very fast disk drive that was touted as a workflow solution. The "workflow solution" arrives, gets unpacked, and is plugged into an existing system. The new piece of equipment is obviously working. The little light is flashing on and off, and it's making that mildly worrisome clicking noise that disk drives make. But is it solving any problems? Is work getting done any faster? Have quality or customer responsiveness increased? The answer to all three questions is probably no. Workflow problems are not solved by just buying the latest and greatest new technologies.

Imagine our friend again who has purchased the new disk drive. But this time, before making the purchase, he researched the workstations in the shop and found that there was one workstation that was processing large image files slower than any other in that department. The supervisor indicated that she considered the cause of the problems to be an old, slow disk drive. So the new piece of equipment becomes a replacement for the slower drive, and now there is an increase in productivity. Though this example may be overly simplistic, it points out an important distinction when considering the relationship between workflow and technology: *Workflow is a plan of action. It is a strategy for how work gets done.*

But if workflow is not a technology issue, then what is it? What are we really doing when we commit to making changes in workflow? Our first thought might be that we're improving quality. But most printing plants already produce quality levels acceptable to their customers and have been doing so for decades. Workflow is a management issue.

It addresses the relationship between throughput, productivity, and profit. Workflow has become the critical issue of concern in the graphic arts because the technological and business environments within which we manufacture our products have both changed enormously in the last ten years. The push for change is coming from influences both inside and outside our businesses, and changing the workflow is paramount to remaining profitable—or just plain remaining in business.

Technology—The Inside Push
Defining how technology has changed the printing industry in the last decade requires an understanding of where we've been. Until about fifteen years ago, printing was entirely within the purview of trained craftsmen. Acquiring the knowledge of printing was like learning some sort of mysterious black magic. It required long apprenticeships and years of training before one was considered to be a master journeyman.

Even then, people were qualified to perform only one task in a series of well-defined roles in the craft workflow. A typesetter produced only galleys of text and display type. A color separator produced only color separations. A stripper brought the pieces together into a final page but had nothing to do with the creation of the individual elements of the job.

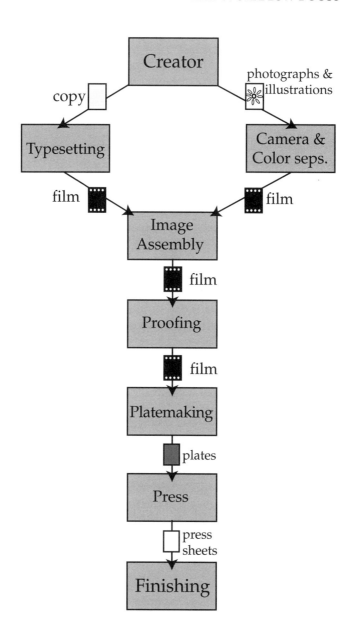

In traditional production workflows, each task was a completely separate operation.

Interdependencies also limited the traditional workflow. A job had to go through the workflow in a set order. Type could not be set until a manuscript had been completely edited. An image could not be prepared until its size had been exactly determined. Assembly could only begin once work on all other elements in a job had been completed. The workflow was controlled by individual artisans who were highly skilled at one aspect of job creation but isolated from the entirety of the job.

Around 1985, three inventions permanently changed the industry:
- The Macintosh computer, which featured an easy-to-understand and easy-to-use interface, was released.
- Adobe introduced the LaserWriter printer—and more importantly, the PostScript page-description language.
- Aldus introduced PageMaker, software designed to run on the Macintosh system, that allowed pages, including images and text, to be fully composed digitally.

Within a couple of years, Linotype had modified one of its typesetting machines (now called imagesetters) to accept and interpret PostScript files, and the first desktop scanners began to be introduced. The digital revolution was off and running, and so were the first workflow problems.

The changes to the traditional print production workflow were immediately profound. Those clearly delineated boundaries between sections of a job were no longer valid. Designers could not only edit copy easily but could also change the layout at will. Typesetting ceased to exist as a viable process and a viable industry, and many of the companies that had previously earned their money in setting type became the first service bureaus, dedicated to outputting fully composed pages of film that designers created, produced, and then sought printout for.

These new and developing technologies no longer fit into the old traditional workflows or job descriptions. Typesetters had to learn the new skills of output specialists. Photomechanical color-separation experts had to become scanner operators. The adoption of new technologies meant that internal changes had to take place within the printing plants themselves.

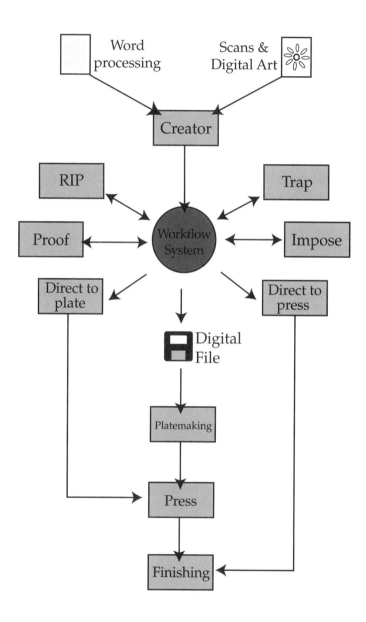

Modern workflows use specialized systems to allow for parallel processes.

Customer Demands—The Outside Push
A major influence on the printing industry is the pressure from customers to meet new demands for manufacturing. Essentially, this can be reduced to four basic requests:

- faster cycle time
- cheaper costs
- higher quality
- more responsive customer service

One of the trends most influencing workflows is the move toward more overall jobs but with consistently smaller and smaller run lengths. Often this can easily double or triple the workload in a prepress department to get the work out the door. Whether a job will run 5,000 or 50,000 impressions on a press, the prepress requirements remain the same.

Other trends toward smaller jobs come from the success of digital, on-demand printing technologies that are able to change the elements on a page for each impression, known as variable-data printing (VDP). Each printed piece is created dynamically by accessing a database whose fields are tagged to represent blocks of text or specialized images.

A related concept driving the move toward digital printing is *distribute and print*, an idea that has seen fruition only with the success of digital presses. An electronic document is transmitted to a printer, who runs only the quantity needed locally in that area. It is a far cheaper solution to e-mail a document across the country than to ship heavy boxes via freight carrier.

Another source of pressure on the printing industry is the increasing demand for consistent, high-quality color. The ease with which color can be generated in a desktop publishing environment has caused more companies, designers, and advertising agencies to insist that printers provide not only traditional four-color process printing but that they also add specialized spot colors or varnishes to the work. Some of the more technology-savvy print buyers and designers are also requesting alternative printing techniques such as frequency-modulated (stochastic) screening and hi-fi (six- and seven-color) printing.

The issue of cost is another pressure forcing workflow changes inside the printing plant. Situations often occur locally in which there may be three or four different companies with very similar equipment. To many print buyers, the only important differentiation between these companies is related to cost. Streamlining the workflow helps companies trim their production costs and increase their ability to provide competitive bids for work.

A final influence from external sources is the request for shorter cycle times in the production of a job. This is driving printers to find alternative methods for proofing. Many printers are turning to soft proofing—that is, using a computer monitor to view a proof—as an alternative proofing technique.

Others are finding it valuable to install proofing devices at the client site. A file is sent via a telecommunications line to the proofer at the remote site, where it is then imaged and is immediately available for review by the client. This "remote proofing" is forcing printers to tackle not only workflow issues but also the telecommunications and calibration difficulties that are inherent in proofing across distances.

Return on Investment vs. Remain in Business
For many years the only reason for a printing company to invest in new technology was to increase the profitability of the company. New technology would be evaluated according to its potential to pay for itself with increased throughput—known as return on investment, or ROI. With the more competitive business environment that exists today, the motivation for many printers to invest in new equipment is based more on the ability to stay competitive by meeting customer demands. This motivation is termed remain in business, or RIB.

Consider remote proofing as an example. In the attempt to meet a customer's request for shorter cycle time, a printer decides to invest in a remote-proofing system to be placed at the client's site. This means not just the investment in the device but also in its maintenance, its supplies, its calibration, its telecommunications link, and internal workflow changes to accommodate a system that efficiently transmits the file to the client site.

Unless the client is very large, it's unlikely that this proofer will directly return enough in sales to cover the investment. It will, however, give the printing company an advantage over its competition by giving the customer a reason not to take its business elsewhere. By making this investment based on an RIB motivation, the printing company has also begun another major trend in the industry—establishing partnerships with client companies to increase the value added from service.

The inherent difficulty of making purchases based on RIB is that ultimately the printing company must recover its investment somewhere in the process. Rather than increasing costs and therefore prices, a better approach might be to work toward streamlining the workflow so that the savings benefit cancels out the equipment investment.

Regardless of solution, these external influences are one of the critical reasons for the move toward workflow reengineering in the graphic arts industry.

The Scientific Approach to Printing
The traditional craftsperson approach to printing has reached the end of its usefulness. Changes in technology, primarily with the adoption of computer-to-plate systems, should not be viewed as an inconvenience around which workflows need to be adjusted. Digital technology, in conjunction with advancements in color science, gives us the opportunity to treat printing with the same set of process controls that are commonly found in other manufacturing industries.

Though it may seem odd to compare printing to an industry like automobile manufacturing, this conceptual shift is necessary if the printing industry is to maintain its profitability as it meets the new demands placed on it. Just like any manufacturing process, the printing industry must take in raw materials, convert them into basic components, and then use those components to fabricate a final product.

In printing, the raw materials of the process are art and digital files (and also paper and ink). These raw materials are then converted into printed press sheets. Finally, the individual sheets are trimmed, folded, and otherwise finished into final products ready to be shipped to the customer.

The trend in the industry toward automation and control of the workflow lends itself well to treating printing as a production process. The use of measuring tools such as densitometers and spectrophotometers allows us to use quantitative rather than subjective measurements to control color and ink film thickness. Many print buyers are beginning to request actual data from a print run to judge whether quality specifications have been met.

The work of standards organizations such as the Committee for Graphic Arts Technology Standards (CGATS), the International Standards Organization (ISO), and the International Color Consortium (ICC), as well as the establishment of published specifications for different types of printing (SWOP, SNAP, or GRACoL), provides uniformity in the requirements of the process so that designers can accurately create artwork that can be used, with limited adjustments, by commercial printers in a predictable and automated manner.

The application of these methodologies to process control in printing is both dependent on workflow and an influence on workflow. In other words, workflow is a two-way street. The integration of the technology needed for process control, like any new technology in a plant, will force changes in the workflow. In contrast, the efficiency and organization of the workflow will directly affect how well a system of process control can be established within the printing plant. Process control is as much a workflow issue as it is a technology issue.

Goals of This Book
This book is designed as a reference for those looking to learn about the issues of digital workflow in the printing industry. Much of the book is dedicated to explaining most of the enabling technologies surrounding digital workflow. There are also sections devoted to methods for evaluating workflows, including the use of flowcharts, profitability effects of reengineering, and the concept of workflow as multiple processes working in tandem.

Technology decisions on workflow require an understanding of print management as much as management decisions on workflow require an understanding of the enabling technologies. A knowledge of both is needed if workflow changes in a printing plant are to be successful.

Chapter 2

Why Digital?

It's impossible to understand digital workflow without knowing the history and effects of digital technology on the printing and publishing industry. The first computers, built in the late 1950s and early 1960s, were technological monstrosities: room-sized banks of transistors and vacuum tubes that had less speed and power than even the smallest hand-held calculators of today.

These computers, known as mainframes, had no mouse or screen to use as an interface. Instead, information was coded by punching holes into cards that had to be hand fed one at a time into a reader. There were no disk drives or other simple ways to store information. A program was loaded into the computer, executed by the machine, and then discarded. Rerunning a program required repeating the entire procedure.

By the late 1960s, there were two new advances in technology that helped simplify computing. Terminals, keyboard units that resembled typewriters, had been added as interfaces. This allowed instructions, or input, to be typed into the system. It also allowed the results of a program, or output, to be typed out onto paper. Magnetic tape drives were also added to the mainframes, which allowed a method of storing and retrieving data.

Before the addition of tape drives, all computer memory was volatile—the information existed only as long as the power was supplied to the computer. Tape drives were the first step toward

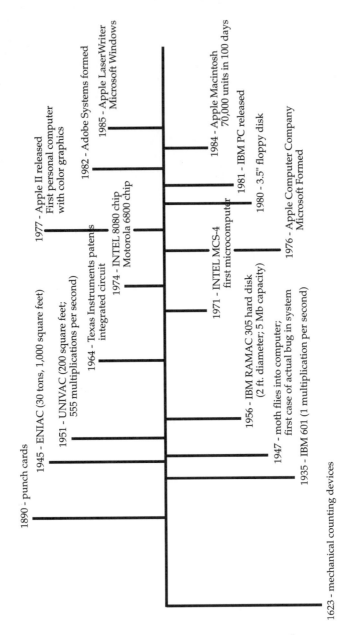

The history of computing devices extends to the seventeenth century.

today's disk drives, or nonvolatile memory. This provided a way to permanently store data so that it could be retrieved at a later date. Despite the addition of terminals and tape drives on mainframes, computers in the 1960s all suffered from the same limitations. They were large, slow, expensive, and difficult to operate.

The invention that really sparked what we know today as the digital revolution was the silicon chip. Instead of transistors and tubes, tiny circuits made from silicon were embedded into microchips. Not only could computers be made smaller, they could also be made more affordable.

There are two main uses for silicon chips, both of which helped enable the use of computers in printing. The first is in the processor itself. Here in the "brain" of the computer, tiny logic circuits enabled the computer to make thousands—and ultimately millions—of computations each second.

The other major advance in silicon chips was for volatile memory. By putting circuits for processing and memory on silicon chips, the microcomputer, or desktop computer, was born.

Monitors, Mice, and Floppies
With the size of computers reduced, other inventions came along that helped simplify computers and make them more practical for everyday use. A monitor, or cathode ray tube (CRT), was added so that first text and then graphics could be displayed for input and output. Xerox's Palo Alto Research Center invented another device that changed the way people interacted with computers—the mouse. By adding a device that would allow users to interface with the computer by "pointing and clicking," operating systems like Windows and the Macintosh OS were feasible.

Another technology development needed before computers could be used for graphics work was improved data storage. Magnetic tape simply had too many limitations to be useful. It was slow and so sensitive to its environment that data could easily be lost. Another problem was that data had to be stored and retrieved linearly on the tape. This meant that as data was added, it could not just be rewritten across the same section of tape. Early microcomputers tried to solve the problem by reducing the size of the tape needed. Pre–Macintosh Apple computers actually shipped with a cassette player that could record data onto audiocassette tapes, but the problems of speed and reliability remained.

The first real fix for the problem of data storage came through the development of a magnetically sensitive disk with a reader head that resembled a phonograph turntable, known as the Winchester disk drive because of its resemblance to a Winchester revolver mechanism. The disk spun at high speed while the read/write head moved just above its surface.

This not only increased the speed and reliability of data storage, it also meant that data no longer had to be stored linearly. The head was free to move very quickly to any section of the disk where the needed data was stored. Though machines today are faster and can hold much more data, the basic mechanisms of today's disk drives are very similar to the original idea—but faster, cheaper, and with more capacity.

It was seen early on that there must be some method for moving information from machine to machine. This inspired the invention of the first removable disks. Similar to the Winchester drives, the reader head was contained in the machine while the data was stored on a removable plastic magnetic disk. Moving data from machine to machine was simply a matter of inserting or removing the appropriate disk. This gave us the terms "hard disk" and "floppy disk"— the permanent internal disks were made from metal, whereas the removable disks were made from a more flimsy plastic.

Even in the early 1960s, developers saw the benefits in being able to connect two or more computers together so they could "talk" to each other. Partly from Cold War fears that computer systems in the United States could be disabled by a nuclear attack, the Defense Department commissioned research that would connect major computers in the country through a network of multiple redundant links. The result was what we call today the Internet. TCP/IP (Telecommunications Protocol/Internet Protocol), the networking language, or protocol, of the Internet, is still one of the most commonly used networking languages. The other major protocol used commonly in the graphic arts is Ethernet, which was developed by Xerox in 1980.

From CEPS to DTP

When we think of digital technology in printing today, we usually are considering desktop publishing (DTP) using Macintosh personal computers. The history of digital technology in printing actually goes back to the 1970s and the first digital scanners. These scanners had analog controls but were connected to a film recorder that is very similar to the imagesetters of today. Light passing through a sensitive photomultiplier tube (PMT) was converted into electronic data and passed on to the recorder, where it was then imaged onto film by a laser.

In 1979, Scitex introduced the first Color Electronic Prepress System (CEPS, pronounced "seps"). Costing nearly a million dollars, this was the first system that allowed images to be sized, color corrected, and placed onto a page. Though the placement of text was not supported, the advantages in time of producing multiple pages of color separations at size and in register pushed many of the largest printers to adopt CEPS technology.

In 1984 and 1985, three releases began the era of desktop publishing. The Macintosh computer was released, featuring an easy-to-use Graphic User Interface (GUI). Aldus Corporation released the first version of PageMaker, software that could be used to lay out fully composed pages of text and graphics. Most importantly, Apple released the first version of its LaserWriter printer, which used Adobe PostScript as its language.

RIPs and PostScript

The effect of the PostScript language on the printing industry was profound. Based on a programming language called Forth that was first developed by Xerox, PostScript allowed pages of graphics and text to be described using mathematics. A PostScript file is device-independent. This means that the specific parameters of the printer—resolution, for example—are kept separate from the actual description of the page. A PostScript file also holds all of the fonts and image information required to reproduce a page. The result is a file format uniquely suited to the graphic arts that can be generated once but interpreted in different ways for different output devices. The same PostScript file can be used to print to a 300-DPI laser printer and a 2,400-DPI imagesetter, taking advantage of whatever features happen to be offered for a respective printer.

Just as important as PostScript was the development of raster image processors (RIPs). The RIP processes a PostScript file and applies the attributes for the printer as it interprets the file. The RIP works by performing three separate operations on a PostScript file. First, the RIP interprets the file and creates a list of all of the elements on the page, called the display or object list. The display list is then converted, or rasterized, to a single file using the parameters of the destination printer. A display list destined for a 300-DPI laser printer is rasterized at 300 DPI. A display list destined for a 2,400-DPI imagesetter is rasterized at 2,400 DPI. Finally, the RIP sends the data to the printer in a language that printer can understand, and the page is imaged by the device.

Development of Imagesetters
Recognizing the potential for using PostScript in the graphic arts, Linotype added a RIP to two of its laser typesetting devices, the Linotronic 100 and 300, thus creating the first imagesetter. An imagesetter is a two-part device: a RIP to process incoming files, and a marking engine to image film or specialized photographic paper.

Imagesetters come in two main types: capstan and drum. Capstan imagesetters were the first type of imagesetter on the market. In these devices the film is drawn through a set of rollers in front of a stationary laser that images the film. The problem with capstan imagesetters is that it is difficult to control the movement of the film precisely through the machine. This results in registration problems for multicolor work.

In a drum imagesetter the film is secured either around the inside or outside of a drum. The laser then moves across the film. The advantage to drum imagesetters is their ability to provide the level of registration needed for multicolor work.

With the combination of personal computer, software, RIP, and imagesetter, desktop publishing began making inroads to high-end printing. Despite the fact that, at the time, front-end systems for color were capable of producing superior quality, and desktop publishing had difficulty with process color, the price differences justified the adoption of DTP systems, both by designers to produce work and by printers to process it.

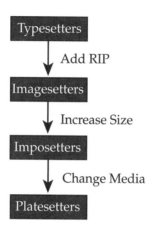

New imaging devices grew from modifications to their predecessors.

Color and Multiple-Page Imagesetters
In 1987, a company called Quark released a page-layout program called QuarkXPress. The program was similar to PageMaker in its ability to compose both images and text into a single layout, with one major advantage: QuarkXPress was capable of creating PostScript output for color separations. Soon after this, the first desktop scanners capable of scanning reasonable-quality color appeared on the market with an image-editing software program from Adobe called Photoshop. With these tools, a designer could now completely create and edit four-color-process work without the need for the expensive Color Electronic Prepress Systems (CEPS).

At the same time there had been rapid advancements both in RIPs and in imagesetters. Adobe had announced the impending release of a new version of PostScript that was more reliable, faster, and better able to handle multicolor work. New imagesetters were also released that could image two-page spreads of four-color process on a single sheet of film. The focus in printing companies began to move away from manual page assembly and toward electronic page assembly.

If two-page spreads could be imaged, then the logical next step was to image an entire form at one time. Oversized imagesetters came on the market that were capable of running sheets of film up to 28x40 inches—large enough to accommodate the maximum sheet sizes of most presses.

These new imagesetters were called imposetters because of their ability to image an entire imposition at one time. New software was also released that could take in single PostScript pages, arrange them, and add any other marks or color control bars that the printer might need. The use of imposetters with imposition software resulted in the first all-digital workflows from designer to film.

Computer-to-Plate (CTP)
Even before the first computer–to–aluminum plate devices had been released, computer-to-plate existed in the printing industry. Polyester plate material with a light-sensitive coating had already been in use with imposetters to provide direct-to-plate solutions. The gravure industry had been using direct imaging engravers to create cylinders since the mid-1980s.

So, though computer–to–image carrier was not really new in the industry, and the technology was in place to digitally create impositions, the task of digitally imaging aluminum plates for lithography posed a new set of challenges.

The first CTP devices, or platesetters, that could image aluminum lithographic plates were flatbed machines. Individual plates were hand loaded and imaged with visible-light lasers. The problem was that the size of the plates was limited, because as the laser imaged further from the center of the plate, the beam of light would become progressively more distorted, ultimately affecting the image quality. The next generation of platesetters were internal drum devices. The plate was mounted inside a drum and the laser moved across the drum to image the plate, much like imposetters.

Though internal drum machines proved successful with visible-light lasers, the development of thermal laser/plate technology caused problems with this design. Thermal imaging uses heat energy instead of visible-light energy to activate the polymerization of the image area on the plate. The advantage of thermal imaging is a much harder dot on the plate, but the problem with an internal drum configuration is that unless the laser is placed directly next to the plate, it requires too much energy from the laser to properly expose the plate. It can be done, however.

The solution was to mount the plate around the outside of the drum and then rotate the plate across the laser. This has proven to be an enormously successful solution. Currently the state of the art in platesetters is the thermal imaging external-plate configuration.

Digital Printing and Direct-to-Press

Beyond computer-to-plate are the families of digital printers and presses and direct imaging presses that continue to be developed today. The first digital printers were an offshoot of digital color copiers. A color copier is essentially two discrete technologies: a scanner section and a printing section. By bypassing the scanner section and sending data directly from a RIP, a color copier/printer can be transformed into a digital press.

A digital press, like Xerox's DocuColor 40, is toner based. Thus it uses an image carrier that is re-imaged for each impression. In contrast, a direct imaging press uses a plate that is imaged directly on the press but does not change from impression to impression.

The Heidelberg Quickmaster DI is the most successful and well known of the direct imaging presses. It gives the quality advantage of ink on paper, while still maintaining the advantages of digital presses. It cannot, however, be used for highly personalized and variable-data printing.

The success of digital presses comes from the elimination or reduction of prepress costs and the ability to affordably print short and very short runs affordably. Many digital presses are used for personalized or on-demand printing—essentially a run of only one piece! Digital printing technology continues to advance. Xeikon's family of Digital Color Presses provided the first high-speed web-based solutions for digital printing. Heidelberg, one of the most respected press manufacturers in the industry, continues to develop both digital and direct imaging presses.

It has been suggested that digital and direct imaging presses are the future of the printing industry. Why? Because they integrate into automated digital workflows more efficiently than traditional printing presses.

Chapter 3

Digital Workflow— Why Now?

Digital technology has been a part of printing for more than twenty years. Why is it that only now we're seeing such an emphasis on digital workflow? Digital technology offers advantages in speed and precision that are a requirement in today's business environment. The integration of new technology requires that printers and designers change some of their fundamental concepts of how work gets done. New business opportunities in Internet and multimedia publishing are forcing printers to reevaluate themselves as communications specialists rather than simply experts in ink on paper. The increase in competition within the industry is moving printers toward the use of digital technology to differentiate their products and services from those of their competitors.

The steady trend toward computer-to-plate has changed the central focus of production work, from manipulating and producing film to manipulating and producing digital files. Any one of these changes could have been accommodated within traditional methods and workflows. But the sheer bulk of the changes and the speed with which these changes have come have forced the industry to reevaluate and reengineer workflow systems. The traditional methods of workflow simply cannot stand up to so much pressure.

Advantages of Digital Technology
The use of digital technology offers a level of precision and control that was impossible to attain using traditional methods. Analog workflows were based on the exposure of materials to a light

source, whether shot in a camera or exposed in a contact frame. Controlling the variables in this process is formidable, and despite the best attempts is always limited in success. How old is a light source, and has its power degraded over time? Is tight contact being maintained between, for example, film and plate? How experienced is the operator, and could that person simply be having a bad day? From creating spreads and chokes to analyzing the color of a press sheet as it reaches the delivery end of a press, analog workflows are prone to the natural variations of light and human nature.

One of the major advantages with digital workflows is in repeatability. We can look at repeatability in two ways. The first has to do with job reruns: running additional impressions of an archived job. Digital press controls that take advantage of density and colorimetry measurements allow exact matches to prior jobs to be achieved. The difference is in qualitative evaluation versus quantitative evaluation. The sheer processing power of computers allows us to mathematically control color and ink density, rather than relying on the skill of an individual operator. The chances of achieving a match are much greater if a press operator is given a specific set of characteristics to match, rather than relying on a visual match of a pre-printed sample.

Repeatability also needs to be accomplished from job to job. All work in a printing plant must go through generally the same set of requirements. Multicolor work, for example, will generally always need to be trapped, proofed, and plated. Digital technology gives us the power to assure that all work from job to job will have the same exposure times and intensities. Imagine the difficulties if no two proofs were ever created with exactly the same characteristics. Even slight exposure variations can affect the color in a proof or the dot structure on a plate. If proofs and plates cannot be controlled, then it becomes impossible to control the process on press. Repeatability removes variation and adds confidence to the process.

Hand-in-hand with repeatability is predictability. Predictability is a major issue in proofing. A proof is useless if it does not accurately predict the characteristics of press performance. In an analog workflow, proofs are made from film. Once film is generated, the only control over the color in the proof is by changing either the proofing colorants or the exposure times used to create the proof. A digital file, though, can be changed endlessly to match different printing conditions by simply manipulating the raw data.

The characterization of processes is also facilitated by the use of digital tools. Colorimetry measurements using a spectrophotometer allow us to precisely measure characteristics of a printing process. But the mathematics involved in color science are very complex. Though colorimetry has been available to printers for many years, it is the processing power of digital technology that allows colorimetry to be a useful tool for characterization. Computerized press controls that use scanning densitometers and spectrophotometers ensure that the process is maintained according to the characterizations.

Linearization and calibration are another arena in which digital technology gives us an advantage. Linearization is the adjustment of a piece of equipment so that its output matches the input values. Linearizing an imagesetter, for example, means adjusting the intensity and the focus of the laser so that when the RIP is sent a 50% value, the imagesetter images a 50% dot. When we calibrate a device, we are typically adjusting that device to match a characterization of a process. This lets us build adjustments for dot gain or ink contamination directly into the system. Successful calibration is only possible if a device is accurately linearized. Digital tools, especially the data in digital files to be manipulated with a computer, give precise and easy control of linearization and calibration.

Computers not only give us more control over the process, they allow us to make adjustments quickly and easily. Characterizing and controlling the printing process is not new, but before computers it was a time-consuming, expensive, and relatively inaccurate process of trial and error. Printers have adopted new technologies not simply because they were available but because by using them they are able to achieve better results in less time and at less cost.

Redefined Roles in a Digital Production Process
As printers and designers adopted digital technology, the emphasis on workflow has also come from the changing roles of jobs and people in the process. Prior to the digital and desktop publishing revolutions, work followed a well-defined path through the

production process. People were trained to perform only one small section of the workflow, and their work had to be completed before the job could progress to the next stage. Going digital meant the elimination of entire industries. It meant that workers needed to adopt new skills, often multiple skills, if they were to remain employable. The typesetting industry is the best example of the effect of digital technology on redefining workflow roles.

Typesetting was an industry that for many years was within the purview of printing. Once a manuscript was written and edited, it had to be passed on to a type house so that the copy could be set in its final form and galleys printed out that would later be placed in position. As desktop publishing advanced in popularity, designers realized that they no longer needed the services of type houses. The job in the workflow of typesetting was absorbed into design.

As typesetters began to realize that their days were numbered, they in turn redefined their businesses. Type houses had one big advantage. Many of them already owned laser typesetting imaging devices—the predecessors to modern imagesetters. Type houses began taking in from designers not manuscripts but files that needed to be output to film. This resulted in the birth of service bureaus, an industry that was created out of desktop publishing. As the new technologies took hold, many of these new service bureaus added services like scanning and design, trying to take back the business they had lost to designers.

With many printers now moving to computer-to-plate systems, the need for service bureaus to provide film is declining. Again, technology has added a solution for service bureaus in the way of digital and direct imaging presses. It is becoming more and more common for service bureaus to adopt these new printing technologies to accommodate the loss of film business.

The modification of the typesetting industry from service bureaus to digital printers is a microcosm of the overall effect of digital technology on the printing industry. Previously well-defined roles in the workflow have been blurred and in many cases simply removed. Likewise, new opportunities for business have been created. The difficulty of this transformation on workflow is in the speed with which these changes have occurred. Type houses were a thriving business only twenty years ago. New workflows not only have to take into account the current state of technology but also have to be flexible enough to change with time.

Internet Effects

Multimedia and the Internet have fundamentally changed the nature of publishing. Printers are faced with a competitor that is virtually free, available to anyone with a computer, and can exceed the limitations of ink on paper by providing resources like sound and movies. The effect of the Internet has introduced a new term to publishing: *repurposing*.

The concept of repurposed information involves reformatting information from one media to another. The information in a printed brochure can be repurposed into a Web site or onto a compact disk. This offers a number of advantages to printers. Printers have a familiarity working with digital files, so a natural extension of business is to offer repurposing services. Just like type houses had to change their business, many printers are beginning to offer their services not just as experts in ink on paper but in all aspects of graphic communications.

The Internet also offers a level of connectivity between printer and customer. Printers can not only offer the service of repurposing, they also can serve as manager of a company's graphic resources. One of the major workflow issues in the coming years will likely be in how printing companies manage the communications assets of their clients. This requires a knowledge of printing, network protocols, and database management, as well as control over how those assets will be accessed by the customer. The Internet is one more way that workflow is being drawn out of the printing plant and into the customer's office.

Effect on Strategic Planning

The adoption of new internal technologies as well as the general acceptance of digital technology by the public is causing printers to rethink their long-term business strategies. It is not enough for a printer to simply print. The trend is toward the integration of services so that the printer can handle all the communications needs of its clients. This doesn't just mean designing a few Web sites. The services of a printer must be marketed within the context of digital technology. Many printers and companies are actively seeking a partnership arrangement. In this relationship, the printer gains the advantage of being a select vendor to a company, while the company receives reduced costs for services as well as the increased efficiency of maintaining all of its communications assets within one vendor. In many cases, printers are subject to inspection and review from the customer before they can be considered for a preferred vendor status.

ISO 9000 certification, a system whereby quality procedures are certified by an independent outside agency, is one of the newer trends in the printing industry. ISO certification provides confidence to the customer that the printer meets a specific level of acceptability in areas of quality assurance, standard operating procedures, and customer-service response. Some larger corporations responsible for millions of dollars of printing each year will not even consider using a vendor unless it has achieved ISO 9000 certification.

In terms of workflow, these new marketing strategies mean that workflow is defined and understandable not only internally but also upon review by a potential client. Workflow is no longer just a function of internal production. To many companies, workflow and its documented procedures are a measure of a printer's capability to produce adequate levels of work.

Film vs. Digital File
The major emphasis on workflow has come as printers have adopted computer-to-plate systems. The critical change is that film, which was always the central focus of prepress production, has been removed from the workflow. Instead of film, the workflow now must focus on the production of digital files. To be successful, workflows must fit their environments. The removal of film has completely changed the production environment in prepress. Traditional workflows simply do not fit the new environment.

Traditionally, every task in the workflow in some way involved the creation or manipulation of film. Text was set and output to film. Halftones and separations were created as random pieces of film.

The collection then moved on to strippers, who arranged all the elements of the pages into large sheets of film, called flats, that represented one or more printing forms. If a change needed to be made, the appropriate piece of film was simply re-created and added, or stripped into, the flats. This gave an enormous amount of flexibility to the workflow. A single change could be accommodated by re-creating only a minimal amount of film.

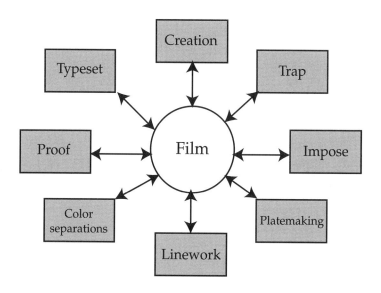

All operations in traditional workflows involved creating or modifying film.

In a computer-to-plate production environment, or in fact any environment in which the image carrier on the press is digitally produced, the flexibility of making changes is removed. In order for the plate to be output, all needed elements must be correctly created and adjusted. Mistakes are more costly in materials.

A single aluminum plate is far more expensive than a single piece of film. Worse, a mistake on a plate may not be caught until it is on press, bringing to a halt the most expensive and important piece of equipment in the factory.

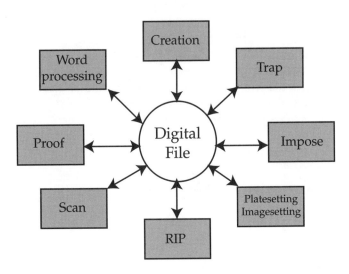

In today's workflow, operations involve the creation or modification of a digital file.

In a plant using computer-to-plate, control of the workflow must go beyond merely accommodating errors. The workflow must be precise enough so that errors are prevented from occurring. And all this must happen within the context of changing roles, new business strategies, new demand from customers, and new technologies. It's no wonder that digital workflow has become the most important single issue facing the printing industry today.

Chapter 4

Standards in the Graphic Arts

What Is a Standard?

A standard is a set of requirements that designers, printers, and vendors follow as they produce and measure work. Standards provide an essential element to the control of workflows. They provide uniformity and reliability by providing a set of guidelines assuring that work produced is portable across companies and countries.

There are standards in the graphic arts covering aspects of work production like screen values on film, standards covering the viewing and measurement of color, standards for the creation of digital files, and standards related to individual printing processes. The goal of standardization is to prevent chaos. Imagine if every state in the United States used a different color of traffic light. How would a traveler going from New York to Connecticut know whether red meant stop, yield, or go?

Standards have become even more important in the digital age where file transmission between states and countries is commonplace. An advertising agency based in New York may now produce work that will be printed at different times in hundreds of locations around the world. The national newspaper *USA Today* is printed in twenty-seven different plants around the country. It would be too expensive and time consuming to produce a different set of advertisement proofs for each plant. Standards provide assurance that work will be repeatable between different jobs and different plants.

Standards also cover measuring and viewing printed pieces. Densitometer and colorimeter standards have been established so that measurements have uniform meaning across the United States, though the European standard for densitometers (Status A) is different than that of the United States (Status T).

One of the most important standards that has been created is for standard viewing conditions. Because color appears different under different lighting conditions, all printed work should be viewed under 5000 Kelvin lighting on an 18% gray background. This assures that when a designer or print buyer looks at a proof, there is consistency in their assessment of the color.

Open vs. Proprietary Systems
Early CEPS systems were known as proprietary or closed-loop production systems. Scanners, processors, and output devices were all a part of a single integrated system. In a proprietary production workflow, the input to the system is controlled completely in-house. All color separations and other page elements are produced by the same company that also prints the final piece.

This gives an enormous amount of control to the printer. Before the advent of desktop publishing and the proliferation of desktop scanners, closed-loop systems were the primary workflows in the printing industry.

The need for standards was accelerated by the adoption of open-loop production. As tasks like color separations and typesetting moved out of printing plants and onto the designer's desktop, problems occurred with a lack of conformance to the characteristics of the printing process. Not only did designers fail to understand the inherent difficulties in successfully creating printable color, scanner manufacturers were marketing desktop devices as able to provide easy, push-button color.

Standards helped desktop publishers by providing them with an understanding of the requirements of the printing process, and helped printers to ensure that materials sent to them from outside the printing plant would conform to needed characteristics.

Types of Standards

There are different categories of standards in the graphic arts. A standard can be related to a single proprietary system or software package. A standard can be based on general acceptance, called a consensus or de facto standard. Or a standard can be voted on and published by one or more of several national and international standardization organizations. Regardless of type, standards always share some characteristics. Standards must be based on practical use before companies will be willing to adopt them. They must also be measurable so that conformance to the standard can be established.

It might seem strange to think of a proprietary standard, but every software package or hardware system involves the use of standards. The native file format for an Adobe Photoshop file is one example of a proprietary standard. Saving a file in this format assures that any Photoshop-specific settings will be included in the file, and that anyone using the software will be able to open the image. Standardized formats also allow third-party developers to have a set of guidelines to work with in the creation of plug-ins or add-ons to the application.

Occasionally a proprietary standard is so common that it becomes a consensual or de facto standard. When Scitex introduced its Color Electronic Prepress System, it used a proprietary image file format called Scitex CT. Over time this format became so popular that other systems and software began to support the format. Adobe PostScript is the most common de facto standard. Even though it is entirely legal for a company to develop its own version of a PostScript interpreter, Adobe's version is generally accepted as a uniform standard. Adobe has even published a set of rules called the Document Structuring Conventions (DSC), which developers can use to be certain that their products are fully compliant with Adobe PostScript.

The most useful standards are those agreed upon and published by standardizing organizations. These published standards give specific rules and conditions for all graphics companies to follow. The two best-known organizations are the American National Standards Institute (ANSI), which administers standards in the United

States, and the International Standards Organization (ISO), which creates and administers standards internationally. Each published standard is given a code or reference number by the establishing body. ISO 3664, for example, references the standard viewing conditions for reflective prints in the graphic arts.

ISO

The International Standards Organization establishes, maintains, and publishes internationally recognized standards. The ISO accepts recommendations for standards from industry leaders as well as other standards organizations. The ISO maintains standards not only for the graphic arts but for many other service and manufacturing industries.

ANSI

The American National Standards Institute is the main body for administering standards in the United States. Unlike the ISO, ANSI does not establish standards. Instead, it takes recommendations for standards from other groups and then takes responsibility for organizing and publishing standards. ANSI also does not limit its activities to the graphic arts.

CGATS

The Committee for Graphic Arts Technology Standards is the main body for establishing standards in printing and publishing. Founded in 1988, CGATS concerns itself only with matters pertaining to the graphic arts. In 1994, CGATS merged with the ANSI/IT8 group (which had itself developed from the Digital Data Exchange Standards) to become the single recommending body for standards in graphic arts technology to ANSI.

CIE

The Commission Internationale de l'Eclairage (International Commission on Illumination) is an autonomous recommending body to ISO. CIE concerns itself with standards for illumination and color science. The foundations for colorimetry are based on standards recommended to the ISO by CIE.

ICC

The International Color Consortium is a group composed of more than forty companies. The ICC's primary goal is to establish and promote a common operating system–based format for color-management profiling. The ICC holds primary responsibility for integrating color management into digital workflows.

Published Characterizations of Print Processes
Advertisers face a unique set of challenges in the printing industry. Rather than producing work for a single set of printing conditions, advertisements are reproduced at multiple locations under various printing conditions.

Advertisers are often unable to determine exactly when and where their work will print until after it is produced. Traditional advertising workflows relied on the advertising agency to produce the work, a set of films for each location, and an accompanying proof. Each printer would receive a set of proofs and films that would have to be stripped into the flats along with multiple other advertisements. The sheer quantity of proofs required for these jobs is still a justification for producing on-press proofs.

The lack of any standardization for the production of advertising films caused chaos in publication printing. Some films had been adjusted for dot gain; others had not. Sometimes films would be provided that had been generated using different screen rulings. Printers found it difficult, if not impossible, to create good color matches to multiple advertisements running on the same sheet but produced under different conditions.

The wide range in the development of digital tools available to create work for the graphic arts was also a cause for inconsistency within production workflows. Applications were released that could render the appearance of a page layout on the screen but which lacked the robust qualities needed to adjust files to a printable condition.

As desktop computers and scanners gained in popularity, the discrepancy between software packages continued (and continues today) to increase. Image-editing programs were another source of inconsistency, with some programs unable to create file formats for color files that would image correctly.

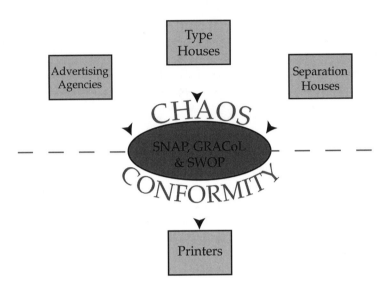

Standards set expectations and turn chaos into conformity.

Specifications for Web Offset Publications—SWOP
By the 1970s, web offset presses had replaced letterpress as the primary method for producing publications. But the problems with uniformity remained. In 1975, the first published standard for a single printing process was released to address the problem. Called Specifications for Web Offset Publications (SWOP), the standard came about from a compilation of publishers, advertisers, designers, prepress houses, and printers.

Their goal was to produce a set of guidelines that would cover all aspects of the creation and production of advertising materials for the web offset publications market.

SWOP gave a measure of predictability to creating advertisements by addressing the needs of all the industries involved in the process. Printers were asked to run their presses to specific densities and characteristics. Prepress houses were asked to produce films at specific screen rulings. This gave designers the information they needed to create work that would reproduce consistently by any printer following the SWOP guidelines.

As technology has changed, so has SWOP. Now in its eighth edition, SWOP has been expanded to cover off-press and digital proofing, formats for digital file exchange, and target colorimetric values for standard SWOP press sheets. SWOP has become so widespread that it is commonly used as a default setting for many image-editing and page-layout applications.

Specifications for Non-Heatset Advertising Printing—SNAP
Obviously, the publications market is not the only place advertisements are printed. Newspapers, which use a non-heatset web process, are another problematic area in print reproduction. The printing characteristics for newsprint have lower densities and higher dot gain values. Inks in this process have different formulations and drying properties. This was not a critical issue in the 1970s when the accepted practice in newspaper production was single-color work with little emphasis on high-quality reproduction.

In the 1980s Gannett Newspapers released the first national daily newspaper that was printed in full color, *USA Today*. Since then, the trend in the newspaper industry has been a steady progression toward four-color process work with an emphasis on print quality. Much like the publications market in the 1970s, newspapers were faced with the same problem from a lack of any conformity to the production of advertising work.

In 1984, the first version of SNAP—Specifications for Non-Heatset Advertising Printing—was released by the Non-Heatset Web Unit of the Printing Industries of America (PIA). Building on the success of SWOP, SNAP provided a similar set of guidelines for the production of advertising materials for the newspaper industry.

SNAP has become the single major specification for newspaper printing. Its last update in 1994 contained provisions for graphics formats, film separations, proofing, and print conditions.

General Requirements for Applications in Commercial Offset
Lithography—GRACoL

Another main market of the printing industry that had problems
resulting from a lack of conformity was the commercial sheet-fed
industry. This increasingly popular type of printing is usually short
to medium runs of high-quality work produced on a variety of
papers.

Problems occurred as desktop publishing systems moved the creation of work out of the printing plant and into designers' offices.
Many designers lacked the fundamental knowledge of print characteristics necessary to produce printed work. Likewise, there was
confusion from the large number of file formats and systems available through desktop publishing.

In 1997, the Graphics Communications Association released what
was called GRACoL as a guideline to lithography processes not
covered by SWOP or SNAP. GRACoL takes a different approach to
the problem by including sections on computer platforms, file formats, correct design, and other attributes that come directly from
desktop publishing.

GRACoL also recognizes the variety of paper types and quality levels inherent in commercial printing. GRACoL acts as a technical tu-
torial for designers, supplying the minimal knowledge necessary to
create printable files as well as a guideline for printing companies
in the production of the work.

Chapter 5

Workstations for Workflow

A workstation is a desktop personal computer that is configured to perform tasks within the digital workflow. A workstation could be devoted to performing just one single repetitive operation, like preflighting, or it could be used for multiple operations within the workflow. The configuration, upgrade, and maintenance of workstations is critical to a successful digital workflow.

Over the years the computer industry has developed its own lingo, and it's important to understand some basic terms that are used to describe computers. Computers are often called platforms and are usually defined according to type of operating system. The term "Macintosh platform," then, is just a computer-nerd phrase for a Macintosh computer. Another term used often is "application," which is just a fancy word for "computer program." So if a computer operator tells you there is a "new application for this platform," the translation is "there's a new program for this type of computer." Don't get thrown off by the lingo!

Central Processing Unit—CPU
At the heart of every computer is a central processing unit (CPU). The CPU is where all of the real work is done by the computer and is made up of the main processing chip, the motherboard, the random-access memory (RAM), the read-only memory (ROM), the video random-access memory (VRAM), and the connecting circuits, which are called buses. There are two main manufacturers of processing chips that we need to be concerned with in the graphic

arts. Motorola makes the chips for Macintosh platforms. Intel makes most (but not all) of the chips for Windows platforms.

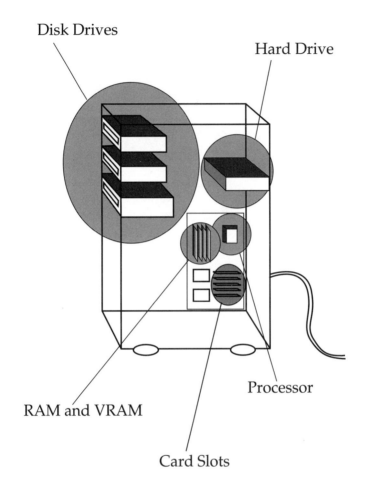

Diagram of computer's central processing unit and drives.

One of the major concerns we have with personal computers is processing speed. The speed at which CPUs operate is measured in terms of megahertz (MHz). You see this all the time in computer advertisements: "New 300 MHz super-computer now for sale!" *Megahertz* measures the speed at which information can be brought into the processor, processed, and then sent back out to the rest of the computer. This is called clock-speed.

Clock speed is not the only measure of a computer's processing speed. Different types of processor chips function at inherently different speeds. For example, the latest processor offered on Macintosh computers is called the G3. Prior to that, all new Macintoshes were sold with 603 or 604 processors. A 233-MHz G3 processor is significantly faster than a 233-MHz 604 processor. Be very careful that you don't rely only on clock-speed as a measure of actual processing speed.

Computer technology changes so fast that it is difficult to publish standards on it. Generally, by the time the book comes out, the information has become obsolete! Consider that just five years ago, in 1995, the fastest clock-speed you could purchase was around 66 MHz. Now it is common to find personal computers that operate at 300 MHz or higher. Suffice it to say that like most things in personal computers, faster is always better.

Random-Access Memory—RAM
Random-access memory is just as important as the CPU speed for computers in the graphic arts. RAM comes on chips that can be easily removed from or added to the computer. There are a variety of manufacturers and types of chips for RAM—SIMM, DIMM, DRAM, SDRAM, and so on. They are not interchangeable, so it's very important that when you purchase RAM you get the specific type that your computer needs.

RAM is also called volatile memory. Information is temporarily stored in RAM and remains there only as long as a program is running. When you run a program, it loads itself into RAM. When you work on a file, it is contained in RAM. If your computer crashes while you are working on a file that exists only in RAM, the data will be lost.

Not having enough RAM is probably the most common error that people make when purchasing computers for graphics work. A normal four-color separation that is 8.5x11 inches can exceed 25 megabytes in size. Adding in the amount of RAM needed for the editing application and the operating system means that in order to efficiently process just that single file, the machine may need to have more than 80 megabytes of RAM installed. Insufficient RAM will have drastic effects on the speed at which work can get done. The best rule of thumb is to fill your computer with as much RAM as you possibly can.

Hard Drives—Permanent Storage
In combination with RAM and the CPU, the hard drive is the third important component of a desktop computer. The hard drive allows files to be permanently stored so they can be retrieved at a later date. Permanent storage is also called nonvolatile memory. When you save a file, you are moving it from temporary storage in RAM to permanent storage on the hard drive.

The unit itself is a magnetic disk that spins at high speeds with a reader arm that moves just above the surface. It looks very similar to a phonograph that plays vinyl records. A hard disk stores and retrieves information slower than RAM. Typically, RAM is measured in nanoseconds while hard drives are measured in milliseconds. Capacities can exceed 8 gigabytes. Additional hard drives are usually very easy to add to a computer.

When purchasing hard drives, take two things into consideration: the speed and the capacity of the device. Higher-speed drives will speed things up considerably when reading or writing large files. Regarding capacity, you should always get the largest drive you can afford. A 1-gigabyte drive may seem limitless at first, but you'll be surprised how fast that space will be filled up with software and images.

Removable Media
A computer does little good on its own. There must be some way for clients to send in files and for graphic arts service providers to receive them. Floppy disks that hold only 1.44 megabytes of data are simply too small to be effective for graphics. This becomes painfully obvious the first time a job is submitted on two dozen floppy disks rubber banded together. Some sort of large-capacity removable disk is a necessity for graphic arts work. There are many options detailed in Chapter 8.

Monitors

Computer monitors can range from small 12- or 13-inch black-and-white devices costing only a few hundred dollars up to 21-inch color monitors costing thousands. Electronic prepress requires, at minimum, a 17-inch color monitor. The reason for this is page size. A 17-inch monitor can display a single 8.5x11-inch page at nearly 100% magnification. A 21-inch monitor can display an 11x17-inch spread at 100%. This is critical for page layout to be done efficiently.

If the workstation is to be used for color correction or image editing, size and color both become issues. Monitors typically have three different ranges of color display to which they can be set: 256 colors, thousands of colors, or millions of colors. Color correction requires that the monitor be capable of producing millions of colors. Size is critical in color correction because in order to accurately render color the image must be viewed at a resolution equal to that of the monitor. Macintosh monitors display at 72 pixels per inch. A 300-dot-per-inch image that will print at 3 inches by 3 inches needs to be displayed on the monitor at 12.5x12.5 inches in order to see the most accurate color!

The monitor, in combination with the mouse and keyboard, is how the operator interacts with the computer, and ergonomic concerns should also be influential in choosing a monitor. Black-and-white monitors cause more eyestrain than color monitors. Smaller monitors cause more eyestrain than larger monitors. Don't forget that someone will be staring at the monitor you purchase for eight or more hours each day.

All too often, companies invest in powerful computers but skimp on the purchase of a monitor. The monitor is just as important as the CPU or the amount of RAM and can often be the deciding factor in achieving accurate color and page layouts.

VRAM and Video Cards

If your intent is to do any high-level color correction or image editing, you need to consider video RAM (VRAM) or a video card in the workstation. These items directly affect the speed at which the computer can render data effectively to the monitor.

If the computer will be used to constantly open and edit images or page layouts, you don't want to have to sit and wait for the computer to redraw the image on the monitor every time you scroll to the next page. This can be a huge waste of valuable production time. Larger monitors have more screen area, of course, and will need more video memory.

VRAM and cards also have an effect on the number of potential colors that can be rendered by the monitor. Color correction on a monitor requires being able to set the device to display millions of colors. This translates directly into more video memory. Video cards and VRAM are relatively inexpensive, and the investment will quickly pay for itself with more accurate color and faster production times.

Peripherals
A peripheral is anything you connect to the outside of a computer. A mouse, keyboard, and external hard drive are all considered peripherals. Peripherals must connect to a computer using a certain type of port. Older computers relied on serial or parallel ports to connect peripherals. These were limited in that the number of devices that could be connected to the computer were limited to the number of ports available. As users needed to connect scanners, CD-ROMs, and multiple removable-media devices, the limitations of using serial or parallel ports were soon reached.

Small Computer Systems Interface ports (SCSI, pronounced "scuzzy") allow users to connect up to seven devices in a series called a daisy chain. Each device in the chain has two SCSI ports. The last device, furthest from the computer, has to be fitted with a terminator for the system to work. SCSI meets all the needs for graphic arts connectivity. It is fast and easy to switch devices in and out of the chain. Newer Macintoshes replace SCSI with the USB, or Universal Serial Bus.

SCSI does have its problems. Though Macintosh computers were shipped with an internal SCSI port until 1999, Windows-based machines require the purchase of an additional card that needs to be installed before SCSI devices can be used.

SCSI use can also tend to be unpredictable at times. Some devices only function when they are installed first on the chain. Occasionally, SCSI devices would cease to function for no apparent reason at all until the chain was reordered. This happened so frequently that an industry slang term, "SCSI voodoo," began to be used to describe the unpredictability of the system.

In 1999, Macintosh and Windows computers began being shipped with the Universal Serial Bus (USB) ports installed. USB offers a number of advantages over its predecessors. USB devices can be connected in a daisy chain using an USB hub. USB is "hot-swappable," which means the computer doesn't have to be turned off to connect or disconnect devices. It has the capability to send electrical power to devices that need it. USB can even be used in some limited network applications. The fact that both Macintosh and Windows support USB means that confusion over device-to-platform compatibility will be reduced. At this point it is fairly certain that USB will replace SCSI and all other peripheral ports.

Operating Systems
The operating system of a computer is the basic software that allows the machine to run programs. It acts as the interpreter, allowing the software to interact with the hardware. Without an operating system, a computer is nothing more than a useless box of metal and plastic. There are three main brands of operating systems that we need to be familiar with in graphics work: the Macintosh operating system (usually called Mac OS), various versions of Microsoft Windows, and UNIX.

The choice of an operating system is what determines all the other decisions about which type of computer to buy. In other words, the choice of operating system drives the hardware purchase. The operating system will determine which software packages you can use and will have serious effects on file portability, the ability to move files from machine to machine.

Macintosh Operating System
If your intent is to do serious graphics or prepress work, then the Macintosh is by far your best choice. This is not a matter of politics or preference—it's a matter of profit. The vast majority of all work

in graphic arts is done on a Macintosh. The Macintosh was designed with graphics in mind, and virtually all of the major desktop publishing applications that exist were first released for this platform. Graphics work done on a Macintosh is simply easier, more efficient, and more predictable. Often this adds up to the difference between making money or losing money.

Much of what drives choices for computers in the graphic arts is compatibility. Files are sent back and forth all the time between companies—fonts, images, and layout files. Many of these files, especially fonts, will not work correctly in the conversion from one operating system to another. If your customers are using Macintoshes—and they probably are—then you need to be using Macintoshes.

Windows 3.1 /95 /98

The Windows operating system comes in three main versions: the now-obsolete Windows 3.1, Windows 95, and Windows 98. Windows is by far the most popular operating system in the world for personal computers. Its introduction was in large part responsible for jump-starting the enormous popularity of personal computing by replacing the confusing, text-based DOS (disk operating system) with a relatively intuitive graphical user interface. Windows machines are also generally less expensive than any other type of personal computer.

Despite its low cost and popularity, Windows suffers from several disadvantages that make it less preferable to use for high-end graphics work. Unlike the Macintosh, Windows was not originally intended to be used for graphics, and support for specialized graphics applications from its manufacturer and software developers still lags behind Macintosh, though adequate software for graphic arts work does exist. This is especially problematic for fonts, PostScript and printer drivers, and system-based color management—critical areas for prepress and graphics.

Though Macintosh still dominates the graphics industry, there is a trend toward more work being done on Windows machines. Many design tasks have been internalized within larger corporations that are unwilling to add Macintosh computers to their otherwise exclusively Windows networks. Support from software developers has increased for Windows graphics applications. The release of Windows 98 saw improvements in font and printer support. As more customers adopt Windows-based platforms for their graphics work, service providers are forced to adapt if they want to stay in business.

Windows NT
Though Windows NT carries the Windows name, it has enough real differences to merit its own category. In terms of stability and speed, Windows NT exceeds any other common personal computing operating system. If you need to use Windows to do graphics work, NT should be your choice.

The advantages with NT come from the way it handles memory. Windows NT has true multitasking, which means the processor can actually be shared between applications. Macintosh and other versions of Windows allow multiple applications to be open at one time, but only one program can use the processor. Windows NT also uses protected memory, so an error in one program will not necessarily affect all other open programs.

NT comes in two versions: NT Server and NT Workstation. Either will function as a stand-alone workstation. Many RIPs and workflow systems use NT Server as their basic operating system, including Heidelberg's Delta system and Harlequin RIPs.

UNIX
The UNIX operating system has been used for decades on mainframe computers and continues to be used successfully today with many graphic arts servers and workflow systems. Though not widely used for workstations, UNIX is the operating system for Silicon Graphics computers and is the basic system for Scitex's Brisque, some other popular RIPs, and specialized workflow management systems.

Despite its stability, UNIX is very unlike the Windows or Macintosh operating systems. If you plan to implement a UNIX-based system, be aware that there is a steep learning curve for the software and that misuse can easily corrupt the system.

Purchasing Considerations
Compatibility tends to be the primary issue in considering the purchase of new workstations. If all of your customers use Macintoshes, you have no choice but to purchase a Macintosh. If you have or expect to have customers using Windows machines, you will need to purchase a Windows machine. Cross-platforming—trying to process Windows files on a Macintosh—will devastate the efficiency of your workflow. Some files, like PostScript Type 1 fonts, simply cannot be cross-platformed.

Unless you're building an entire department from the ground up, the new workstation will also have to be compatible with the existing network system. Most graphic arts businesses use some form of Ethernet as their network protocol. Though support for this is built into Macintosh computers, it will usually require the purchase of an Ethernet card if you are adding a Windows machine.

The speed of the machine will be directly affected by the type of processor and amount of RAM installed on the computer. It used to be common to walk into electronic prepress departments and see employees reading magazines while they waited for their workstations to process files. Buy the fastest processor available. The difference in cost will be quickly made up in faster production time. The minimal RAM requirement for graphics work is 128 megabytes. If the workstation will be used to drive a scanner or for color correction, you will probably want to double that amount.

Other things you will have to consider are the size of the hard drive and any VRAM or video card requirements. Graphics files are larger than in any other industry. When you consider that often just a single job takes more than 1 gigabyte of disk space, the purchase of an 8-gigabyte hard drive is justified. Assess what the workstation will be used for before you start shopping. With a little planning you can buy computers that arrive preconfigured and ready to be integrated into the workflow at your shop.

Chapter 6

Networks— The Tie That Binds

A network is a group of two or more computers connected in such a way that file transfer is possible. Individual computers on a network, called nodes, "talk" to each other via a specific language, called a protocol. Standards exist that govern the appropriate cabling and connectors to be used in a network. Ethernet is one of the most common networking standards used in the graphic arts. Graphics work poses unique networking challenges because of the sheer bulk of the files being transmitted. Very few industries commonly deal with files that exceed even a single megabyte in size, but in the graphic arts it's common to have files many times that size making multiple transmissions across a network.

The network can be thought of as the vascular system of a digital workflow. It provides the connectivity needed to move jobs between workstations and servers. Unfortunately, the network is frequently the greatest source of bottlenecks within a company. An efficient network needs to be carefully planned, implemented, and maintained. Most printing companies, however, lack the resources to keep a full-time network specialist on the payroll. Thus, networks within the printing industry tend to suffer from lack of planning and lack of maintenance. Instead, these networks are a jumble of cables that have been haphazardly stretched from machine to machine as the company grows.

Networking is enormously complex, and it's impossible to cover in any depth within a few pages. Nonetheless, there are some basic fundamentals to networking protocols and topology that should be understood by everyone working with the system on a daily basis.

Speed

Network speed, also called bandwidth or throughput, is a measure of how much data can be sent across the network in a specified time. Speed is normally measured in megabits per second, abbreviated Mbps. The speed of the network can be affected by multiple variables, including the type of network, number of nodes, level of activity, type of cabling, and even the size of the files themselves. Thus there is usually a difference between rated speed, which is the maximum possible throughput, and actual speed. The difference can be enormous; in some cases actual speed will be only 33% of the rated speed.

Packets

When a file is transmitted across a network, the entire file is not merely streamed at one time from the sending station to the receiving station. Instead, the sending station divides the file to be transmitted into smaller sections called packets. Each packet contains a section of the file, plus a header and trailer that gives information needed by the receiving station to reconstruct the file. Packets are sent one at a time across the network. Once the sending station receives a message that a packet was successfully retrieved at the receiving station, the next packet is sent. When all packets have been sent, the receiving station then reassembles the file into its previous format.

LocalTalk

Networking is one of the many things that is built into Macintosh computers. LocalTalk is a networking protocol that allows two or more Macintosh computers to be easily networked. Though there are serious speed limitations, LocalTalk is worth mentioning as an example of how the Macintosh computer has played such an integral role in the development of digital workflows in the graphic arts. Many networking solutions within printing companies began with very simple LocalTalk networks. LocalTalk is generally an unacceptable network solution because its low throughput (1.5 Mbps) will not give the speed required for an efficient workflow using even small graphics files.

Ethernet

The other network option that is included with most Macintosh computers is Ethernet, by far the most widely used networking standard in the graphic arts. Developed in 1980 at Xerox's Palo Alto Research Center, it was never really intended for graphic arts use.

Ethernet comes in a variety of forms, the most common of which is called 10baseT. All Ethernet systems follow the same naming conventions. The "10" represents rated throughput in Mbps. The "T," or any number that takes its place, represents the longest cabling segment that can be used in 100-meter increments.

In this case, the T means that the longest segment of cable connecting two stations is limited to 100 meters. Following this naming convention, 10base5 Ethernet means an Ethernet network with a rated throughput of 10 Mbps and a cable-segment limitation of 500 meters. Each type of Ethernet also has particular cabling associated with it. For instance, 10baseT requires unshielded twisted pair cabling; 10base2 requires coaxial cable.

The problem with Ethernet is the way it handles packets. In an Ethernet network, only a single packet at a time can be transmitted across the wire. Each packet is considered to "own" the network. Though this is not a problem with very small networks, as more workstations are added and try to make multiple transmissions, the packets begin to collide and interfere with total network throughput. Eventually, the number of collisions can result in a chain reaction of errors that brings the Ethernet network to a screeching halt—a situation known as a broadcast storm. Collision solutions usually involve dividing the network up into finite smaller sections, thus limiting the number of workstations on any one section.

There are a number of varieties of Ethernet that have been and continue to be developed. Fast Ethernet (100baseT) has been adopted by many larger printing companies. Though it requires an additional card to be installed in a computer, it improves rated throughput to 100 Mbps and still uses the same cabling as 10baseT Ethernet. Recently a version of Gigabit Ethernet was released that further improves the throughput of Ethernet networks.

TCP/IP
Telecommunications Protocol/Internet Protocol is commonly used by many of the larger workflow systems. As its name suggests, TCP/IP is the language used for Internet communications. Like Ethernet, TCP/IP divides a file into packets, but it includes an address for the receiving station in the header of the packet. Because individual packets do not need to own the entire network, this results in an increase in actual network speed. TCP/IP can be used along with Ethernet as a networking solution in larger shops, where TCP/IP is used to connect segments that will carry a large amount of traffic.

Hubs, Bridges, and Routers
One of the most common methods of avoiding throughput degradation in networks is to divide the network into smaller finite sections, called segments or zones. This limits the ownership problem of Ethernet packets to the number of nodes that are on the zone. This is similar to the telephone system in the United States, which is subdivided with area codes for large geographic regions and then further subdivided to individual exchanges (the first three digits of a seven-digit telephone number). Dividing a network into segments requires the addition of devices that serve a function similar to telephone switchboards.

The simplest extension to a network is a hub. A hub does not divide the network into segments. Instead, it acts just like adding an extension cord to an electrical outlet: It's a central device into which several workstations can be connected. This can help in overcoming the distance limitations of Ethernet cabling. A switched hub is a slightly smarter device that allows discrete connections to be made between a transmitting and receiving node within the segment. Essentially, this sets up a mini-network within a single network segment while a transmission is taking place. Using a switched hub can help to avoid the packet-collision problems of Ethernet without subdividing the network into segments.

A bridge is a device that divides a network into segments and allows communications to take place between segments. Where a hub may have ten different nodes connected to it, a bridge might have only two hubs connected to it. Users can make requests to the bridge to allow access across the bridge to another segment of the network. A router is a smarter bridge that not only allows access across segments but can also read the header of individual packets and point them directly to the intended receiver station. The intent with routers and bridges is to limit the number of packet collisions that tend to quickly degrade network throughput.

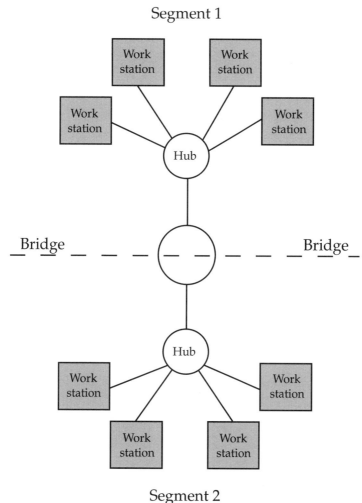

Networks are segmented using various specialized connectors.

When To Call an Expert

Networking in most printing plants suffers from a lack of planning. As a company grows, solutions like Ethernet are gradually added, often without taking into account issues of cabling length, proper segments, and network topology. The systems "expert" for the company tends to be one of the output or imaging technicians, simply because they are the people closest to the computer technology.

This is really not surprising, considering how complex networking issues are and how expensive it can be to call in expert help from outside the company. In every case, however, as a company grows beyond its abilities to handle networking solutions in-house, the need develops for at least one full-time information systems expert to be employed by the company. Unfortunately, this usually doesn't happen until the network performance has become so degraded that it is having serious effects on the efficiency of the workflow.

Entrusting an output technician with the responsibility to create and maintain the network is one of the most serious errors that a printing company can make. Though output technicians may be perfectly capable in knowing how to plug several computers together with simple connections, most of the time they lack the education and expertise required to properly assess the throughput and topology requirements of the company as a whole.

An inefficient network will always result in an inefficient digital workflow. It is common in the industry, especially among mid-size printing companies, to find situations where it actually takes longer to get the job on and off the workstations than it does to perform print-related work on the job. If anything close to this is happening, it's time to call a networking expert. Despite the costs, bringing in outside help in the form of a consultant or full-time employee will quickly pay for itself in increased production time.

Chapter 7

Servers

What Is a Server?

A server is a computer on a network that acts as a central storage or processing station for all of the workstations on the network. In contrast to individual workstations, which can function with or without a network, use of a server requires, by definition, the use of a network. Servers can perform a number of different functions in support of the workflow. Some servers act solely as large, centralized storage devices from which workstations can access files. Other servers assist in routing files to specific destinations on the network.

The role of servers is critical to the efficiency of a digital workflow. As centralized storage areas, they allow jobs to be worked on at multiple workstations while avoiding the duplication of files or jobs. Servers facilitate the organization of jobs in a printing plant by providing a single location for storage. Servers can also be used to add automation to the workflow—a function that becomes one of the most important elements in controlling the flow of digital files through a printing plant.

Generally, the focus of a server is very different from that of a workstation. With workstations, the focus tends to be on processing speed. Servers, which in many cases act as very powerful disk drives, focus on input/output (I/O) speed. Servers in the graphic arts fall generally into three different categories: file servers, print servers, and workflow servers. Each will be discussed in depth.

The Client/Server Relationship

Individual stations on a network that can access a server are called "clients." This relationship holds true regardless of the size of the network. The Internet is an excellent example of client/server relationships. When users enter addresses into their browser, they are actually sending requests out across the network for a particular server to send them the requested files. The server processes the request and then transmits the files. Functionally, all client/server relationships follow this request/transmit structure.

Some servers are designed to maintain applications that can be shared by multiple clients at one time. These applications servers are not widely used in the graphic arts. The sheer bulk of the files involved places too much processing demand on the server station. There is also the potential for files to become corrupt or, in cases where a stringent document-management strategy is not in place, for incorrect and uncontrolled multiple versions of the same file to be created.

Macintosh Servers

Though servers have different functions than workstations, they still basically have many of the same components as any computer. The choice of operating system for a server must be based on a slightly different set of criteria, including ability to connect to multiple devices, speed, and ease of use. All major vendors of workstation operating systems also have server variants of their systems.

Though it would seem likely that Macintosh servers would dominate the graphic arts industry because of their established prominence as workstations, this is not the case. Vendors of RIP and workflow systems have developed most of their software systems around other operating systems.

The advantage to Macintosh servers lies in the familiarity that printing companies already have with the Macintosh operating system. Macintosh servers have drawbacks in speed and memory management that make them generally unsuitable for heavy use as servers; however, the heavy brand loyalty that exists to Macintosh in the graphic arts industry means that we will continue to see these servers being used.

Windows NT
Windows NT is without a doubt the most common server operating system in use in the printing industry. Windows NT combines the general familiarity that most users have with the Windows interface with impressive stability and memory-management functions. Unlike Macintosh, Windows NT allows true preemptive multitasking—the ability for the processor to share its resources with various applications. Because of this, Windows NT is an excellent choice for workflow servers, which commonly automate several tasks in the production workflow. The limitations of Windows NT occur when a large number of users—more than thirty—try to connect at one time.

UNIX
Though UNIX servers are just as reliable and powerful as Windows NT–based servers, they lack the familiarity that exists with the Windows or Macintosh interfaces. Many printers are reticent to add the learning curve for UNIX to the already difficult issues of establishing an efficient network and workflow in their plants.

UNIX exists in many different forms depending on which type of hardware is chosen as a server. Silicon Graphics machines use a form of UNIX called IRIX. Some workflow servers, however—most notably the Scitex Brisque system—require the use of UNIX as a server operating system.

Novell NetWare
Though Novell is one of the more common types of servers found overall, it has not achieved popularity in the graphic arts industry. Overall, Novell is a well-established system that offers high-speed access and excellent security features. The price for this is a level of complexity that exceeds the limits that most printing plants are willing to chance.

Novell is difficult to set up and difficult to maintain. Using a Novell system virtually requires the addition of a full-time server and networking expert to the company's staff. Though this might be acceptable for the largest printing plants, the majority lack the resources to afford this level of expense. Novell remains strictly a high-end solution.

File Servers

A file server acts as a central storage device from which workstations can access and share jobs or images. The advantage to locating all jobs on a central server is that it becomes easier to control job duplication and updates. Document-management software, strategies, or procedures can be used to ensure that only one version, the latest version, of a job will exist at any given time.

In the confusion of organizing fifty different jobs being worked on at a dozen workstations at any given time, a file server provides the minimum safety net required to control the work in progress within a digital workflow. Some companies that have recently installed a file server system have found that they no longer need the vast majority of the hard drive space they originally purchased for their workstations.

The requirements for a file server involve focusing on input/output speed more than processing speed. Because few if any applications will ever be run on the file server, the speed of the processor need only be fast enough to support keeping up with the network. What becomes very important is the speed at which files can be read to and from the hard drive of the server, as well as a network connection fast enough to support multiple transmissions of large graphics files.

One variation of a file server commonly seen in the printing industry is a dedicated image server. Because continuous-tone graphics files commonly exceed 20 megabytes in size, it makes sense to maintain a separate server optimized to store and transmit large files. Image servers are usually used in concert with an OPI workflow. Open Prepress Interface (a modified but similar system is called APR by Scitex) avoids excessive network transmission of large files by automatically creating low-resolution copies of images that can be placed into page layouts as FPO (for position only) files.

When the page-layout file is printed, the server automatically replaces the low-resolution proxy files with the high-resolution version maintained on the image server.

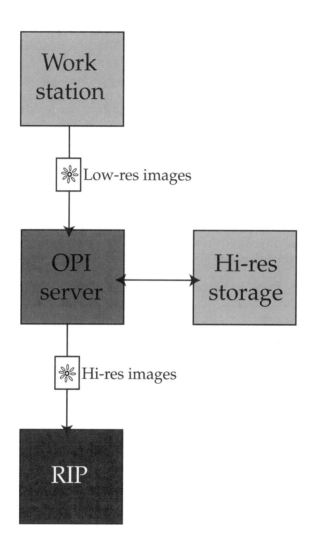

OPI reduces the burden on a network by storing large files on a special server.

Print Servers

A print server acts as a traffic-control device for production environments that have several printing devices. They provide automation to a digital workflow.

To understand how a print server functions, imagine a plant that has two imagesetters, two laser printers, and a digital proofer. Even though there are five total devices, an operator only sees three choices as a printer selection is made from the workstation: imagesetter, laser printer, and proofer. The print server receives the job and routes it to the appropriate device. Print servers are also "smart" enough to recognize which devices are busier than others.

If imagesetter A is already processing a job, another incoming job will be routed to imagesetter B. Another capability of print servers is to share a job across more than one device. In this case. if a four-color job was sent to the imagesetter queue, and both imagesetters were free, the print server might route the cyan and magenta plates to imagesetter A and the yellow and black plates to imagesetter B.

If OPI is to be used in the workflow, it usually becomes the responsibility of the print server to manage the proxy swaps from low-res to hi-res files. It is common to find print servers and file servers working in concert with each other across the network to provide maximum system functionality. Often these two servers are connected by a separate dedicated high-speed network. Selectively creating specialized high-speed connections between devices that commonly exchange high-resolution files is a method for increasing overall network performance without completely replacing or upgrading the existing infrastructure. The automation provided by a print server in combination with OPI has immediate benefits to a digital workflow.

One of the biggest encumbrances to workflow efficiency, especially in terms of network traffic, is the large file sizes of color images. In most "office" network environments, files transferred across the network are measured in kilobytes. In the graphic arts we measure files in tens of megabytes. Fully imposed forms could represent hundreds of megabytes of data. An OPI solution can effectively limit the number of network transfers needed for these files.

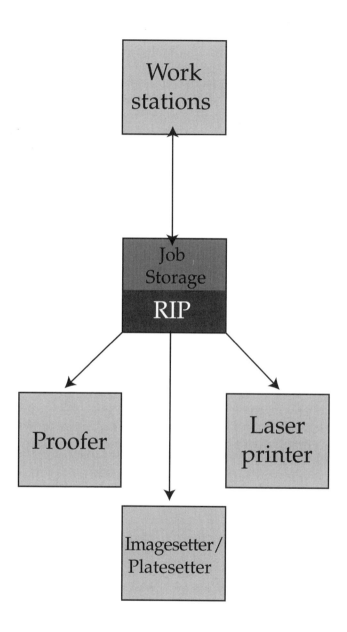

Some servers combine multiple functions in one box.

Applications Servers
An applications server maintains programs that can be activated and shared by its client workstations. In this system, a workstation connects to the applications server and launches the appropriate program. The program interface functions on the client machine, while the bulk of the processing takes place on the server. Where file and print servers require an emphasis on I/O speed, an applications server must have the processing ability to run different programs or different versions of the same program all at one time. Successful applications servers solve this problem by multiprocessor systems (systems using more than one processing chip) and by preemptive multitasking.

Workflow Servers
Workflow servers are the most powerful tools used to control digital workflows in the graphic arts. They combine features of file servers, print servers, and applications servers in one concise system that allows full automation and job control to be added to the workflow. Workflow servers are typically purchased as one unit from a vendor and are designed specifically to support the proofing, imaging, and platemaking devices that exist within a single printing plant.

The advantage to combining an applications server with a print server is that repetitive tasks that must occur in the production cycle can be routed by the print server as needed. Entire workflows can be programmed into the workflow server and set up as printer queues that operators can access from the client stations. Workflow servers can be capable of handling OPI, trapping, imposition, color correction, RIPing, and job routing.

To understand the power of a workflow server, consider that most jobs in the prepress production cycle must go through the same set of steps. A four-color job, for example, must be imposed, trapped, proofed, and then imaged if the proof is approved. A two-color job might only need to be imposed, trapped, and imaged. Using a workflow server, each set of tasks can be programmed into the print server, which will then route the job through the applications and file servers as needed. The only operator intervention needs to be in the initial choice of workflow path through the system.

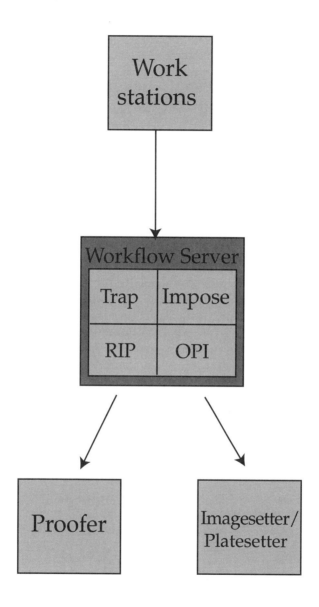

Workflow servers perform print-related operations in a central location.

Including the RIP as a part of the workflow server adds even more power to the system by being able to incorporate late-binding changes through the server rather than forcing the job back to the starting point on the workstation. Task integration and routing are discussed in depth in Chapter 16.

Server Backup and Maintenance
Realizing the role that servers play in the digital workflow should immediately imply the importance of proper maintenance and backup. The task of maintenance should fall within the same purview as network maintenance. The server is the backbone of the workflow; every job in the plant will need to travel through the server at some point. A poorly maintained server will cause job errors and cycle-time slowdowns. Worse, lack of maintenance could contribute to system errors or crashes resulting in job loss. Server maintenance cannot be stressed enough.

Likewise, all jobs on the server should be backed up at least once per day. At any given time, hundreds of thousands of dollars worth of work could reside on the server. The loss of this data will cause irreparable damage to the plant. There are many strategies for proper backup. Software systems like Retrospect can be set up to automatically back systems up across a network to a variety of media including DAT or CDs.

The use of RAID (redundant array of independent disks) technology can also provide enough redundancy to quickly recover from a crashed system. Whichever backup strategy you choose, you must take into account that eventually the system will crash, and your work must be protected from this eventuality.

Server Security
Security plays an increasingly important role in print shops. High-end customers often demand that their jobs, which may contain sensitive proprietary information, be protected from unwanted access. There is also an increasing trend for printing companies to allow their customers a certain amount of access to their internal systems through the Internet. Often customers can log onto a printer's system and access exact scheduling and delivery information for their jobs.

Server security falls into three main categories. The first is the use of user names and passwords for access. Though this may be adequate for internal use, these systems constantly suffer from people's tendencies to write this information down. A computer system has no way to verify that a password has been stolen or is being used without authorization.

The second level involves the use of firewalls. A firewall system applies levels of security to data in a system and then limits access above an approved level for users. Firewalls in concert with a user name/password provide multiple levels of security to the server.

Filtration is a third level of security that creates finite sections of a system. Users can access only certain areas of the system. This is useful if a Web-based interactive system has been set up so that customers have the ability to access information from the printing plant about their job.

The best security solutions combine multiple levels of security. This can be extended to include differing levels of security based on the specific connecting computer. Connections from within the company may require only a password to establish access. Internet connections, however, can be forced through other security systems.

The trend to create Web-based systems is increasing the need for security concerns. The Internet's advantage is in the ability of people anywhere to easily connect, but this increase in freedom comes at the price of network security. Companies need their Web presence to be accessible to the public yet still keep sections of the site open to certain users.

Where customer access is concerned, the server security should not be excessively overt. People suffer from an excess of passwords, and aside from carrying them around with them—a generally bad idea—it is difficult to remember every password associated with every account. One solution is to use systems that can record information about the account directly onto the connecting client's hard drive. Though not popular with computer anonymity purists, this is an effective way to keep security systems from being encumbrances and allow proper access without undue burden.

Security concerns come not only from outside the company. A disgruntled employee familiar with a company's computer systems can cause far more damage in a shorter time than hackers coming in across the Internet. The best security systems combine all three levels as appropriate to the system.

Chapter 8

Storage

Need for Storage

When a program is run or a file is opened on a computer, the data gets loaded into random-access memory, located on chips inside the CPU. Early computers were able to run only a single program at a time. Punch cards or paper tape containing the program was fed into the machine, and after the program was completed it was discarded from memory. Rerunning the program meant going through the whole process again of reloading the program.

The same problems existed with generating output from the computer. Mainframes could be set up with units to punch tape or cards so the data could be retained, but there was no easy way for a person to interpret or do any further work with the information. The problem resulted in hundreds of cards and rolls of paper tape that had to be carefully stored. If even one section of the tape or a single card was damaged, the entire set of data would be unusable.

Developers realized that for computers to become more user friendly, there would have to be a better way to store and retrieve data. Magnetic tape seemed a viable option, and drives were developed that could mount reels of tape and read or write the data just as we use audiocassettes today. Though this was better than punched cards and paper tape, it was still a bulky solution, and the data could easily be lost from problems with the storage environment. Magnetic tape was also slow because the data was written sequentially on the tape. If the program was at the end of a reel of tape, the user would have to fast-forward to the exact spot of the beginning of the program.

The problems with tape storage led to the development of the first hard drives. These devices were made of disks coated with a magnetic substance that could be spun at high speeds. A reader head could float across the disks just above the surface, reading or writing data. The first hard drives were slow and enormous compared to today's standards. The disks were 2 feet in diameter—bigger than entire computers are today—and could only store 5 megabytes of data. Still, they were a huge improvement over magnetic tape.

Even with hard drives, the problem still existed of moving data from computer to computer. If computers were going to be useful to people, the data would have to transportable to a different machine or location. In the 1970s, the first floppy drives were invented. These devices used a mechanism similar to hard drives, except a thin plastic disk was used instead of metal. Though these first disks could only hold 64k of data, that was enough to fit files that contained text or numeric data. Just as important, it was an affordable alternative that could be manufactured small enough to fit into the first desktop computers. For the first time, software and data could be sold and transported cheaply from machine to machine.

As time went on, floppy disks got smaller and could hold more data. The first floppies were made of flimsy paper and were 5.25 inches in diameter. In the early 1980s, the 3.5-inch format that we still use today was developed. These disks could hold more information in a smaller format and, because they were encased in plastic instead of paper, were less subject to being damaged. As the disks got smaller, though, files got larger. As computers became more of an everyday item and more software options developed, files went beyond just containing text.

In the late 1980s, as desktop publishing developed, the need for larger storage devices became a major issue. Hard drives that could hold only 30 megabytes of information could be filled up in a matter of days with layout files and software. The first Macintosh computers didn't even have a hard drive at all! There were only two 3.5-inch floppy drives. The system software would go in one drive, and files could be saved on the other.

The need for expanded storage devices was really pushed as desktop scanners were developed. A typical text or layout file is only a few hundred kilobytes in size and can easily be fit on a floppy disk. But even black-and-white scans of printable resolution exceeded the capabilities of a floppy disk. Where a text file is measured in kilobytes, image files are typically measured in tens of megabytes. For a document to be created entirely through desktop publishing, there had to be larger options.

Desktop publishing required not only that the files can be saved on a hard drive, but the files had to be moved somehow to the printer or service bureau for output. Devices needed to exist that could hold the contents of an entire job and could also be moved from location to location.

Removable Hard Disks and SyQuest
The first company to come up with a solution that served the needs of desktop publishing and the graphic arts community was Sy-Quest. SyQuest drives were truly removable hard drives that could hold up to 44 megabytes of data on a sturdy 5.25-inch plastic disk. SyQuest drives were affordable, and the units were easy to connect to computers. By the early 1990s, virtually every designer, service bureau, and printer supported SyQuest drives. In time, the company expanded the product line by releasing larger formats of the media in 88- and 200-megabyte sizes.

Companies' experiences with SyQuest drives underscored another critical aspect with the use of removable hard drives. In order for the system to work, both the sender of the files and the receiver of the files had to own at least one of the units. To be successful, a removable drive system had to be adopted by multiple users—in effect becoming a de facto industry standard. This made it difficult for other companies to compete with SyQuest and break into the market for large-format removable drives. For several years in the early 1990s, SyQuest remained the single supplier of removable-disk options for the graphic arts market simply because everyone had already spent the money on the units, and their jobs were already stored on SyQuests.

Magneto Optical Disks

Magneto optical disks were one of the early contenders for a share of SyQuest's market. MOs, as they were called, were a smaller 3.5-inch format that could hold just over 100 megabytes of data. Not only were MOs smaller and capable of holding more data than most SyQuests, but SyQuest users began realizing that SyQuest disks tended to be a bit unreliable. Too often a designer would send a job on SyQuest to a service bureau only to get a call the next day that the disk could not be read.

Even more frustrating was the fact that the same disk that could not be read at the printer's office worked just fine at the designer's office. This was only a minor inconvenience if the service bureau or printer was across town. But if the files had been shipped across the country, it could delay jobs for days at a time.

As designers began trying MO disks as an option, printers were also forced to buy the MO drives. If even one of their clients purchased an MO, a printer was forced to buy the drive just to keep that customer's business. This started a process that continues today in which designers tend to drive the choice of devices that printers and service bureaus purchase.

Though MO drives never achieved the popularity of SyQuests in the United States, and their use has all but died off here, they were important because they were the first real challenge to SyQuest's hold on the market. MOs continue to be used in other countries, however, where they achieved much greater success.

Iomega ZIP

In 1995 a company called Iomega released a new removable-drive product, called ZIP, that was directly marketed to the graphics art business. The drives were compact and easy to connect to computers, and the disks were in the familiar 3.5-inch format but able to store up to 100 megabytes of data. ZIPs became popular almost overnight and were the first removable hard drive system to really pose a challenge to SyQuest. Within a year not only were ZIPs found in every prepress and design house, but versions of the drive had been developed to support running on Windows (the original drives were released only for SCSI, which was primarily a Macintosh connection system), and manufacturers of desktop computers began offering the drives as internal options for machine configurations. ZIPs continue to be one of the most popular options for removable hard drives in the graphic arts.

Iomega JAZ (and the end of SyQuest)
The single limitation to the ZIP system was that its capacity of 100 megabytes was often too small to fit entire printing jobs on a single disk. By 1997 Iomega had released another system called JAZ, which was capable of holding up to 1 gigabyte of data on a single disk in a 5.25-inch format. Supported by the established popularity of ZIPs, JAZ drives were immediately implemented by many design firms that consistently produced jobs that could not be transported via a single ZIP disk.

To compete with ZIPs, other manufacturers had tried to market systems that offered greater capacity than 100 megabytes, including SyQuest, which was still trying to recover from its loss of market share to Iomega, but none was as successful as the JAZ system. By 1998 SyQuest was driven out of business by the success of Iomega.

CD-ROM
In the late 1980s, the compact-disk system for audio recording was standardized as the method for digital recording. Compact disks are made of plastic with a metallic coating on one side. A laser is used to etch a pattern of pits into the plastic material. A CD reader reflects a laser off the etched disk and is able to replay digital data that has been stored on the disk.

Because the data on a CD is digital, computer and software manufacturers realized that this would be an excellent storage format. CDs can hold up to 650 megabytes of data on a single disk. Because the system is optical, one of the greatest advantages to the CD format is its longevity. If cared for properly, the data on a CD is estimated to be secure for up to 100 years.

CD-ROM (read-only memory) specifies a type of CD that contains prerecorded data. At the outset of CD technology, the lasers and machines required to etch the disks were too expensive to be marketed to the general public. CD-ROMs can be played back but cannot be recorded onto.

As compact-disk drives became more popular for use in computers nearly every manufacturer offered as standard an internal CD drive on their computers. It is virtually impossible to find a new computer today without a CD drive. Software manufacturers have also moved to releasing their products on CD. For many popular desktop publishing programs, ordering floppy disks for installation requires the user to pay an extra charge.

CD-R

As technology for producing compact disks developed, the lasers required to etch the disks became smaller and were able to be manufactured cheaply enough to be marketed to the general population. Ever since CD-ROMs had been released, it was obvious that to be an effective method for storing and transporting jobs, CDs needed to be recordable on site. In 1996 the first CD-R (compact disk— recordable) drives were released. Though the first devices were expensive, within a year the price had dropped to the point where users could easily afford CD-R drives for desktop use. It is now possible to purchase a CD-R drive as an internal device with new computers.

CD-R had immediate practical uses in the graphic arts for large-capacity permanent storage. Entire collections of high-resolution images are commonly stored on CD-R. CD-R is also widely used as a method for permanently archiving printed jobs that may require reprints at some point in the future. Though CD-R has not replaced the Iomega systems for day-to-day transport of jobs from designer to printer, it has established itself as the best format for long-term permanent storage.

DAT

Prior to the use of CDs, digital audiotape (DAT) systems were used to record digital data for both audio and computers. Though DAT has a large capacity of up to 4 gigabytes of data per tape, it still suffers from the same limitations as other tape-based storage systems. The data is recorded sequentially on the tape, which means the user has to fast-forward through the tape to find the beginning of the needed data before it can be retrieved. Digital tape systems are also subject to the danger of losing data from environmental conditions, tape wear, or device malfunction. DAT is still used in the industry but solely as a long-term archiving system. DAT is almost never used to transport files from designer to printer, and the widespread adoption of CD-R systems threatens DAT with obsolescence.

DVD
Digital video disk (DVD) is the newest format for recording digital data. A DVD works similar to a compact disk with some new innovations. DVD uses MPEG compression to fit more data on a smaller disk. DVD is also etched with two layers of pits instead of one, essentially doubling its base capacity. Though DVD is still so new that it has not permeated the graphic arts market, the format has the support of all major manufacturers of compact disk and digital recording equipment. DVD is likely to supplant CDs as the major format, not only for computer data but also for audio and video digital applications.

The Connectivity Nightmare
As new removable drive systems were introduced over a period of years to the market, printers found themselves in the unenviable position of trying to support receiving files on SyQuest, ZIP, JAZ, MOs, and CDs. Printers and service bureaus were simply in a position in which to offer their services to their clients, they had to be able to receive digital files. This led to a mess of different drives and systems that had to be somehow interconnected just so files could be entered into the production workflow.

Over the last few years, many companies have simply given up on adopting every new system of removable drive. It is common and acceptable now for printers and service bureaus to publish lists that set limits on supported formats for removable disks.

Sneakernet
Sneakernet, a slang term adopted by the graphic arts industry, represents a "network" that relies on removable disks, rather than

standard networking, to transport files from workstation to workstation inside a shop. As graphics files got larger, existing networking systems that were based on the ability to transmit relatively small files could not move files fast enough to keep up with the workflow.

SyQuest disks were frequently kept in-house for transport because the networks were so slow. With solutions like 100baseT Fast Ethernet now available as an affordable alternative, and with the increasing use of centralized file servers, sneakernet systems are rarely used anymore inside companies.

Backup and Archiving
As capacities for removable disks got larger, these systems were used for backup and archiving of jobs. As any common computer user is thoroughly aware, computers are notorious for crashing, usually at the worst possible time. The disks inside hard drives spin at exceptionally fast speeds, and the reader head is constantly moving from location to location to read or write data. This means that inevitably any hard drive will ultimately fail and all the data on it will be lost. Removable disks, which production companies had already purchased to support their customers, offered an affordable and easy way to protect systems against crashes.

It is important to differentiate between the terms "backup" and "archive." Backup is a temporary copy of work in process to avoid the loss of information from a disk or system error. Backup is a protection strategy against the inevitable mechanical failure that occurs in computers. All workstations and servers in the production process should be backed up on a regular schedule—daily, if possible. Even the loss of a single day's work can cost a company many thousands of dollars.

Companies are often lulled into a false sense of security because fatal disk crashes do not happen on a regular basis. This is why it's important to establish a set of standard operating procedures for backup. Some companies rely simply on the operator manually copying files to an external storage device at the end of each workday. The regular stresses of production work make this a bad idea. Will the operators take the extra thirty minutes to back up files on days when they have just completed an extra two hours of overtime? Even the best employees will tend to skip over this process occasionally.

A far better system is to use automated backup software linked to a separate workstation dedicated solely to the task of backup. An older computer that may be too slow for file processing is a perfect candidate to be used for backup. The processing speed of the backup station is irrelevant; it need only support a fast network connection, have a backup device connected to it, and be able to run the appropriate software. Automated software can be preprogrammed to back up other workstations across the network at night when overall traffic on the network is at its slowest.

Archiving is the permanent storage of work after the job has been completed. Printed jobs often go through a cycle of reprints as the customer needs more of the product. Archiving a job allows the printer to recall the needed files that have already been finalized and adjusted to match press conditions. Traditionally, plates and films were archived using a file system. Entire rooms could quickly be filled with old plates in the traditional system—a waste of valuable space that could be devoted to production-related equipment. In a digital workflow, it makes more sense to simply archive the files that were used in the creation of the job, then store them on a bookshelf!

The choice of exactly which files should be archived is an important decision that must be made about the strategy. Should only the original files be stored, or should the PostScript and imposition files be stored as well? What about the RIPed, or rasterized, bitmap files that exist on the workflow server?

Though this decision needs to be made on an individual basis, it's safe to assume that at the very least, all original, PostScript, and imposition files, as well as all images that may reside on an OPI server, should be archived. Archiving the rasterized bitmap files, which are large in size and usually cannot be adjusted once created, will be useful only if the printing conditions in the shop stay consistent between the time the job is originally run and the time any reprints are ordered.

Likewise, there may be times when the original imposition might need to be changed. Since any change renders the rasterized bitmaps useless, it makes little sense to waste space saving these files.

Another issue involved in the archiving strategy is the choice of medium that will be used for storage. Three options exist that are viable for archiving printed jobs: DAT, CD-R, and DVD. Other options are eliminated based on either limited capacity or the risk of data loss. DAT is a popular system because the tapes are inexpensive, less than 50 cents apiece, and can hold up to 8 gigabytes of data. The biggest problem with using magnetic tape systems for archiving is the potential loss of files. If tape is going to be used, a second copy, essentially a backup of the archive, needs to be made so that data permanence can be assured. This doubles the time required for archiving.

CD-R is a better system, even though the disks are more expensive and can hold only a maximum of 650 megabytes. The payoff of CD-R is reduced archiving time and the security of knowing that the data is virtually permanent. DVD may ultimately be the best option for archiving digital files; however, right now DVD is so new that it may be wise to wait for the technology to mature before committing to its use for archiving.

Just like backup, archiving needs to be approached with a formal set of procedures outlining the process. Often, the same workstation and software used for backup can be used for archiving. This allows both the backup and archiving processes to be condensed into one manageable, automated solution. Once established, an efficient storage system should only require operator intervention when the media needs to be changed in the drives.

Legacy and Obsolescence
One of the biggest problems faced in any work involving computers is that the constant and rapid development of new technologies means ultimately we will be faced with owning equipment and systems that are obsolete. The term "obsolete" represents anything that has outlived its usefulness. In digital terms, this usually means a technology that has been superseded by a newer and better technology.

Consider the example of SyQuest. Even though the company no longer exists, many thousands of jobs still exist on SyQuest disks. Companies must still occasionally dust off their aging SyQuest drives to handle these situations. Ultimately, ZIPs and JAZ drives will fall into the same category. Obsolescence needs to be carefully considered in the purchase of new systems. DAT systems currently face the same threat from CD-R and DVD.

Another term for obsolete equipment, files, and systems is "legacy." Legacy media must be addressed in the storage and transport of digital files. This needs to happen before the equipment becomes so old that it ceases to function and the data can no longer be retrieved. One good strategy that few companies use is to schedule time to move files from legacy media onto a more current format. Though a client may find forgivable that your company no longer supports equipment like SyQuest's, having old jobs that cannot be retrieved due to lack of planning for obsolescence is unacceptable.

Internet Effects on Transport Media
The general trend for removable drives has been toward smaller sizes, higher capacity, and higher stability of the media. This has been driven by the need in the graphic arts to transport files from designer to service bureau or printer. Though it is unlikely that this trend will reverse itself, on-line transmission is having an influence on the need for removable transport media, which will probably result in less emphasis being placed on the development of new systems.

Early applications of the Internet were generally unacceptable for file transport in the graphic arts. Modems were too slow to transmit large jobs. Many files were sent as e-mail attachments, which resulted in problems since the e-mail system was never designed to handle large, multiple files. Users were also unfamiliar with Internet connection standards and languages. It was more preferable to put a disk in the mail than to spend all day waiting for a file and find that it had been corrupted in transmission.

As companies like WHAM!NET market secure, fast, and easy connectivity solutions, file transmission is becoming the rule rather than the exception in the graphic arts. Not only are designers sending more jobs to the printer on line, proofing options like soft and remote proofing are requiring the printer to transmit files back to the designer for approval. As file transmission becomes more commonplace, the need for hard-disk media to transport files will be reduced. In the future it is likely that more emphasis will be placed on the use of removable media for efficient backup and archiving than for job transport.

Chapter 9

File Formats
and Digital Art

An efficient digital workflow revolves around the manipulation and control of digital files. Throughout its life cycle, a document will need to go through many transformations before it is finally committed to an image carrier. The creation of a document brings together text, images, and illustrations into a single layout file. The combined layout file is then subject to even more conversions as it is imposed, proofed, and imaged. Each step in the process has its own special requirements that generate an individual file type. Text files from word-processing programs are far different from color-separated CMYK files that come from a scanner. A large part of workflow problems come from a failure to understand and use each file type properly.

File Type vs. Art Type
One of the easiest mistakes that novices to digital art make is to confuse the distinction between the type of file that is used and the type of artwork that is represented by that file. Artwork can be separated into four finite categories:

- text
- images
- illustrations
- layouts

All four types of artwork can be saved into a multitude of different file types, though we will learn that each type of art has certain file formats that work best for a particular type of art. Never make assumptions about what the file contains based solely on the format that is used to save it. An Encapsulated PostScript file, for instance, could hold an image, illustration, or complete page layout. If in doubt about the type of artwork that a file contains, always double-check by opening the file or asking the creator of the document.

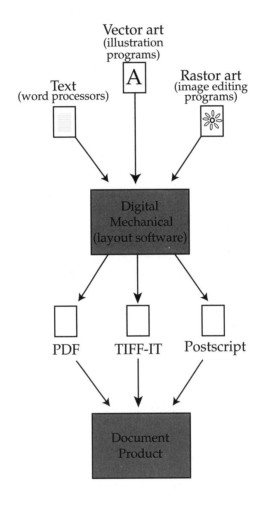

A document can go through many stages in its life cycle.

Native File Formats

Every program used in the creation of a digital document has a single proprietary file format associated with it. When a document is written in Microsoft Word, it is saved into a file format designed exclusively to be used by Microsoft Word. Adobe Photoshop files can be saved in the Adobe Photoshop format. We generically call any file that is in the proprietary format of its creation application a native file format. Native file formats are how you should save any work in process because they are designed to hold any attribute that has been assigned to the document by the program. Word files, for example, are designed to remember the text, indents, and type of font used, whereas Photoshop files remember whether image layers have been used.

Native file formats work only as long as we continue to use them with the original program. But once work has been completed on part of a document, it must be passed on to the next stage of the process in a standard format that the next program can read. An illustration created in Adobe Illustrator needs to be converted from Illustrator format into Encapsulated PostScript before a page-layout program will be able to import the file.

Text Files

Whenever a document is created, part of the process is to write the copy or text of the document. Usually the author isn't interested in the final layout of the document; the concern is primarily with writing the copy. A word-processing program designed specifically to facilitate the needs of writing copy should be used to create text. The two most popular word-processing applications are Microsoft Word and Corel Wordperfect.

Once the copy is finished, it needs to be converted from its native format into a format that allows the text to be placed into a layout program. Text files are the simplest files used in the graphic arts. The standardized format for text is ASCII (pronounced ass-key). ASCII represents text by placing it into a 7-bit binary format that can be read by virtually any program in existence. Any word-processing program has an option that allows the document to be saved in an ASCII or text-only format.

When you do this, notice that the program usually warns you that saving it in this format may cause certain attributes of the document to be lost. This is because when we convert from the native file format to ASCII text, we lose everything except the character representations. Doing fancy pagination in the word-processing program is pointless if the file will need to be converted to text-only before it goes to the next stage of the production process.

Raster and Continuous-Tone Art
Black-and-white or color photographs that need to be reproduced are called continuous-tone art. The term "continuous" represents the fact that these images have gradual variations in tone from light to dark, similar to what we see in real life. Another term for this type of artwork is "raster art." In imaging terms, a raster represents one line of data in an image. Continuous-tone images are represented by a three-dimensional grid of pixels that give the file its resolution, bit depth, and color depth. Each of these attributes contributes to the reproduction capabilities of the image.

Raster art is built from a grid of pixels.

Resolution

Continuous-tone files are resolution-dependent; the ability of the image to reproduce properly depends directly on the resolution of the image. *Resolution* is defined as the number of pixels that exist in 1 inch of the file space. Typically, resolution is referred to in dots per inch, but this is incorrect terminology. Dots are attributes of output devices. When talking about continuous-tone images, we should use the designation pixels per inch (PPI) or samples per inch (SPI).

The choice of resolution is based on the intended screen ruling of the final reproduction. The formula to use to determine the correct resolution of a continuous-tone image is:

(screen ruling) x 2 x (reduction/enlargement percentage) = image resolution

If we have an original that will be enlarged 200% and printed at 133 lines per inch, the correct resolution would be:

133 LPI x 2 x 200% = 532 PPI

The same image reduced by half would be:

133 LPI x 2 x 50% = 133 PPI

The reason resolution is so important to image reproduction is because we need to give the imagesetter enough data to accurately create halftone dots. The "2" in the formula represents what we call the quality factor of the image; it controls the pixel data that the RIP will use to create halftone dots. Optimally, we want the RIP to use four different pixels to create a single halftone dot, which we achieve with a quality factor of 2. Using less resolution means that the RIP has to share pixels to create halftone dots. If the quality factor drops below 1, the RIP cannot differentiate tone between two consecutive halftone dots. The result is a printed image that lacks tone and detail.

Because of the relationship between size and resolution, once an image has been scanned it cannot be enlarged without sacrificing reproduction quality. This is the limitation of using resolution-dependent images. If an image at 300 PPI is scaled up to twice its size, the new working resolution of the image is now 150 PPI. Though it is possible to resize images in an editing program like Adobe Photoshop, to do this the program has to create new pixel data based on an average of the existing pixels, called interpolation. The result of interpolated resolution is never as good as the original resolution, so for best quality all images should be originally scanned at the needed resolution for the printing conditions.

Scanning an image without enough resolution causes noticeable problems.

Bit Depth
Each pixel in an image represents a certain tone value. Because this data is digital, the number of available tone values is always some exponential function of 2, ranging from 2(1) power (1-bit, two possible values) up to 2^8 power (8-bit, 256 values). Though certain scanners are capable of capturing data up to 2^{12} power (12-bit, 4,096

values), these images usually need to be converted back to 8-bit values before they can be processed by the raster image processor.

The bit depth controls the number of variations that are possible for each pixel to hold. All photographs should be represented in 8-bit. The human eye is capable only of perceiving less than 200 discrete variations of tone from white to black. Though it may be possible to print images in greater than 256 levels of gray, it only serves to add greater size to the already large files we use without really achieving any perceptible increase in reproduction quality.

Line Art
Line art is a special type of raster image that shares some but not all attributes of continuous-tone images. Line-art images always have a bit depth of 1, called 1-bit images. Each pixel has only two options: It can be turned completely off, representing white, or turned completely on, representing black. Another name for line-art images is bitmap, because the pixel layout represents an on-off map of bits. Line art is used whenever a solid, single-color element needs to print. Type and many logos are represented by line art.

Line art has special requirements for resolution. Generally, line art should always be at the same resolution as the output device. If the final piece will be printed on a 300-DPI laser printer, the image should be at 300 PPI. The only time this cannot be adhered to is when the resolution of the output device exceeds 1,200 DPI, which is the case for any imagesetter printing at screen rulings beyond 100 or so. Just as the human eye can perceive only a limited number of tone variations, there is also a limit to the amount of detail we can see.

The human eye cannot perceive resolution differences beyond about 1,200 dots per inch, so we set that as the maximum needed resolution for line art. From a practical standpoint, it makes sense to play it safe and assume that all line art needs a resolution of 1,200 PPI.

Just like any resolution-dependent image, scaling line art proportionally changes the resolution of the image. In fact, it is very easy for the eye to perceive line art that is at an improper resolution because of the harsh contrast in the image.

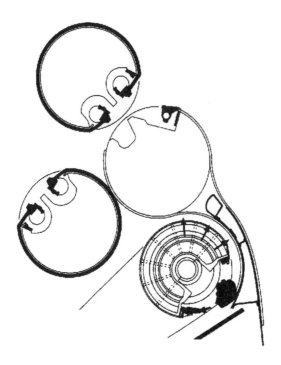

Line art must be at the resolution of the output device in order to appear crisp.

Color Depth

The easiest way to understand color images is to think of them as a number of single-color images overlaid on top of each other. In a halftone, or single-color image, resolution determines the number of pixels, and bit depth determines the total number of tone variations to each pixel. In a color image, each discrete color is just like one single-color image.

A four-color CMYK image is essentially four different single-color images, with each one designated to represent cyan, magenta, yellow, or black when printed. Each color in these images is called a channel, so occasionally color images are called multichannel images.

The exact same limitations as far as size and resolution apply to multicolor images as apply to single-color images, so the same formulas are used to determine the resolution in terms of the final printing size of the image. Overall, however, resolutions for color images are much higher than for single-color images because the data must be represented for each color. An RGB image will be three times greater in size than a single-color representation of the same image—three channels instead of one to get the red, green, and blue. A CMYK file will become 133% of the size of its RGB equivalent—four channels instead of three.

File Formats for Raster Images
Despite the variety of options that exist for file formats in saving continuous-tone or bitmap artwork, there are really only two file formats that should ever be used with files intended to be printed: TIFF or EPS. These are the only image formats that save all the data needed for high-end reproduction.

TIFF, or Tagged Image File Format, was originally created by Aldus in the 1980s. Since then, the format has gone through a number of revisions that have standardized the format. TIFF files can contain line art, grayscale, RGB, or CMYK data without loss from compression. TIFF is supported by all major applications for electronic publishing.

Occasionally a continuous-tone file needs to be saved with special attributes attached to it. Silhouettes, or clipping paths, may need to be used to outline certain sections of an image. Spot colors might need to be added to the image. Sometimes specific transfer curves or screening options need to be applied to the image. If any of these is a requirement for a special-case reproduction, then the file should be saved in Encapsulated PostScript (EPS) format.

An EPS is a special kind of PostScript file that can save data using mathematical representation of outlines. Because EPS is a subset of the primary printer language used in the graphic arts—Post-Script—it is supported by all high-end applications.

One special type of EPS file that is seen occasionally is the desktop color separation (DCS) file. DCS files are multiple-file formats. Saving a CMYK file in the DCS format will result in a five-part file: one file for each color plus a composite low-resolution master file. If spot colors or special plates are a part of the image, they will be added as a separate file. DCS files were popular several years ago because the pre-separated images were faster to print than composite images. With the availability of affordable OPI solutions to the industry, though, DCS is now limited to special-case uses.

Digital Illustrations and Vector Art

When we create a drawing in a digital illustration program, what we're in effect doing is instructing the computer to write a complicated series of commands that mathematically represent the visual image we see on our monitor. The computer uses a very powerful page-description language called PostScript.

PostScript uses mathematics to represent outlines, or vectors, of objects that are composed of points, lines, and objects. Specific color attributes can be applied to the outlines and contents of vector objects. When we create a square in Illustrator, what the computer actually creates is lines of text that, when interpreted by a machine that reads PostScript, can reproduce that square.

Vector art has a number of very important differences from raster art. Vector art is resolution- and device-independent. Because objects are represented mathematically, individual characteristics of a printing device are not applied until the file is processed by the RIP. This means that the exact same file can be used to print to a 300-DPI laser printer or a 2,400-DPI imagesetter, and the artwork will always be reproduced at the highest resolution and quality level that the device supports.

A related attribute to resolution independence is that vector illustrations can be scaled to any size without loss of data. Remember that raster art was limited by its resolution—enlarging a piece of raster art by 200% results in a 50% loss of resolution and image quality. Doubling the size of a piece of vector art tells the computer to in essence multiply everything in the file by 2, but because resolution is not applied to the file until printer processing, there is no loss of resolution. There is no limit to this scaling potential. The same piece of vector art can be used on a piece of letterhead and then used to fit on a billboard without any loss of quality.

Vector at 300%

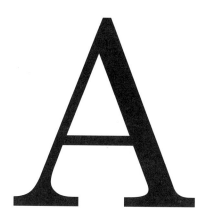

Raster at 300%

Enlarging raster art without increasing resolution distorts the image.

Another advantage to using vector art is that there is no limit to the number of edits that the artwork can go through. In raster files, every time a change is made, some pixel data is lost to the image. Repeated edits to a raster file can cause the color to look fake—as if it was created by a computer (which in fact it was). With vector art, each time an edit is made, the computer simply rewrites the mathematical formula that represents the image.

In comparison to all raster art, vector art files are much smaller. An 8.5x11-inch raster separation at 300 DPI (standard for most printing applications) is more than 25 megabytes in size. A piece of vector art the same size might only be a 25th that size. This can be a huge time savings when transporting files on disk or across a network.

Using Vector Art

Just because vector art has certain advantages over raster art does not mean that it is always appropriate to use it. Vector art is excellent for images that have distinct solids, crisp lines, and spot colors, but it cannot reproduce the fine tonal variations that occur in life-like images. This means that vector art is perfect when used to represent logos, maps, or graphs but should not be used to represent an outdoor landscape or portrait of a person.

Another disadvantage of vector art is that even though the files are smaller than raster files, they use very complex mathematics. Occasionally a complicated, troublesome vector file can slow down or even crash altogether a printer's RIP. This becomes especially problematic when vector files are placed inside other vector art files, called file nesting. Whenever creating complex vector graphics, it is always wise to cut and paste elements from one piece of artwork to another, rather than importing or placing one illustration into another.

File Formats for Vector Art

Whenever vector art has to be saved from its native format into a transportable format, Encapsulated PostScript should be used. EPS is the only format that will save all the information about the file that is needed by both the RIP and the page-layout application. Choosing any other format will cause problems at some point downstream in the process. Though this may change in the future—there are indications that PDF (see the description of intermediary file formats on the following page) may ultimately be a replacement format for EPS—right now EPS is the only choice for saving vector art intended for high-end printing.

PostScript Files

Once all the elements of a document—text, type, illustrations, and images—have been created, they must be arranged to form the final document, called page layout. The most common programs for page layout are QuarkXPress and Adobe PageMaker. The result is an electronic mechanical that must go through further processing before it will be ready to print. The next step is the creation of a PostScript file from the page layout.

PostScript is one of the key technologies that allows electronic publishing to exist. It is a standardized programming language that is designed to represent page information. It converts visual elements like type and objects into mathematical information that can be read by multiple printers. This makes it possible for a user to create a document, generate a PostScript file, and then distribute that file to the printer with all elements in place.

Original digital workflows were PostScript workflows. Single-page PostScript files were at first imaged to film and manually stripped into place on the printing form. As larger imagesetters were released, PostScript workflows changed. Instead of imaging single pages, the PostScript files themselves were imposed digitally and then output as a single piece of film (a flat) ready for proofing and platemaking.

The complex mathematics that makes PostScript so powerful is also the reason for its biggest problem. As the RIP interprets the PostScript code, there are many places where errors can be made. A single missed number or command could cause the entire document to fail to process, generating what is called a PostScript error. As pages became more complex and printers attempted to push the limits of PostScript, the problem of PostScript errors caused inefficiencies in the workflows. It became obvious that although PostScript was a powerful language, some amount of preprocessing was required to ensure that pages would image correctly at the RIP.

Intermediary Files

Many current workflow systems use intermediary file formats to simplify PostScript files before they are processed. Intermediaries act as a buffer between the PostScript pages and the RIP. PostScript files are interpreted, but instead of moving directly to the imaging process they are stored in a different file format. Some workflow systems use intermediaries that are proprietary. They can be used only by the system that generates them.

Other vendors have chosen to use one of two standardized intermediary file formats: Adobe Acrobat's PDF, or a version of TIFF called TIFF/IT.P1. The advantage of using a standard intermediary is that the file can be used for proofing or imposition with a large degree of confidence that the intermediary accurately represents the final look of the document.

Another advantage of intermediaries is that they are created beyond the interpretation stage of the RIP process. More than 90% of all file errors occur as PostScript errors in the interpretation stage of the RIP.

After interpretation, the RIP generates an object list, also called a display list. The display list is different from the original PostScript file in that it represents a number of discrete objects that are accessed via a lookup table.

There is some controversy over the exact meaning of the statement that intermediaries do not need to be "interpreted." The argument follows that because PDF is still in ASCII or binary format, it does need to be interpreted at the RIP. The problem is in defining what we mean by "interpret."

A PostScript file is a computer language, and like any other language it must be interpreted from source code with the results of the program in part determined by the RIP's setup. A PDF does not need to be interpreted in that sense. Instead, device-dependent attributes are applied to individual objects, which can be accessed through the look-up table. This feature is what allows PDF to be a device-independent form of file transfer.

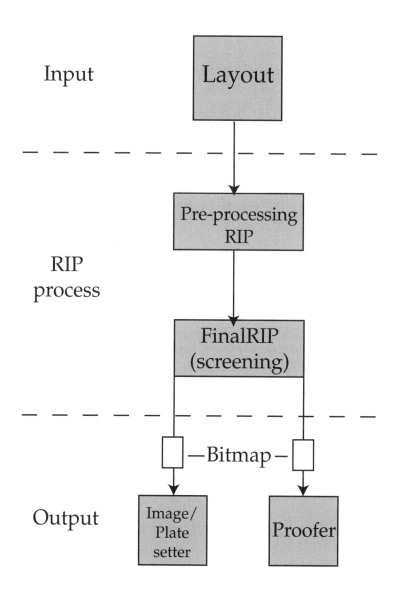

Intermediaries are created by partially RIPing incoming files.

Adobe PDF

In 1994 Adobe Systems released the first version of its Acrobat Portable Document Format (PDF). PDF was not originally intended for high-end graphic arts use. It was originally marketed as a file format that could transfer documents across multiple computer platforms without losing the integrity of the page. It made no difference whether the document was created on a Macintosh, Windows, or UNIX platform—any user could open any PDF file.

Acrobat worked under a two-part system. The Acrobat Reader software was used to open and read a PDF file. Reader was freely available to anyone who wanted a copy of it. To create PDF files, it was necessary to use Acrobat Distiller. What became a critical motivation for the use of PDF in printing was that Distiller required a PostScript file before it could create a PDF.

The appearance of PDF virtually coincided with the printing industry's realization that intermediary file formats were a necessity in a digital workflow. Since PDF was already PostScript based, using PDF for high-end printing was a logical next step. The use of PDF has been held back because it was never intended to be used to create high-resolution page data. As Adobe realized the potential for PDF, it offered two quick updates that made PDF high-end capable. PDF is poised to become the primary file format in the graphic arts. PDF 1.3 is due to be released and will include many fixes to the format geared to the high-end graphic arts user.

Even more important, the Committee for Graphic Arts Technology Standards (CGATS) has approved a version of the format, which will be called PDF/X, or PDF/Exchange. PDF/X directly addresses the needs of high-end users while at the same time excluding items like sound and movies that are unnecessary in graphics work. The establishment of PDF/X as a published standard for file exchange will add the final level of confidence to using PDF on a common basis for the graphic arts industry.

TIFF /IT

TIFF/IT, Tagged Image File Format/Imaging Technology, is an expansion on the TIFF standard designed to increase its usability within the world of high-end image processing. TIFF/IT is based on file formats introduced years ago by Scitex, one of the world's leaders in imaging and graphic arts systems. A TIFF/IT file is composed of three different data files: CT (continuous tone) for the actual pixel data of the image, LW (linework) for high resolution (usually exceeding 1,000 pixels/inch) data, and HC (high-resolution color) to define high-resolution edges to CT data if needed for trapping. These three files are then linked through a fourth FP (final page) file.

TIFF/IT is not widely supported in the United States at this time, though it has seen some use in Europe. Most users of TIFF/IT are in the deadline-intensive publications market, where the issue of digital integrity in a traditional PostScript workflow (where files are subject to differing interpretations through different RIPs) has created the need for a more reliable image standard. Predictions lean toward the ultimate choice of PDF rather than TIFF/IT as the intermediary file format most likely to see widespread use.

File Formats for Multimedia and On-Line Documents
The growth of the World Wide Web (WWW) has caused a huge demand for documents to be published via network and has raised new dilemmas for graphics file formats. Put simply, none of the file formats acceptable for printing can be used for network publishing, and none of the formats acceptable for network publishing can be used for printing.

When a file needs to be printed with ink or toner on paper, the critical elements are that the format supports high-resolution color data with no loss of integrity. For Internet or multimedia documents that are intended primarily to be viewed on a monitor, the size of the file is much more important.

Even though modems and connection speeds are consistently getting faster, the idea of downloading a 20-megabyte color image from a Web server is still impractical. The selection of image formats for network publishing is driven primarily by file size. Images must be as small as possible so that users with small bandwidths can still maintain an acceptable access time. To this end, file-compression algorithms used for these formats are "lossy"—quality is sacrificed to achieve the smallest possible file size.

Another critical issue in network file formats is browser compatibility. Markup-language documents are dependent on the browser for interpretation and display, thus any image format unrecognizable to the browser cannot be displayed to the end user. The two major WWW browsers, Netscape Navigator and Microsoft Internet Explorer, limit image support to two types of files: JPEG (also known as JPG) and Compuserve GIF.

JPEG (Joint Photographic Experts Group) files contain raster data and are characterized by a lossy compression algorithm. This allows them to achieve various amounts of compression with a proportional amount of image degradation. Though this is unacceptable for the printing industry, network documents are usually intended to be viewed only on a computer monitor. All browsers support JPEG files.

The Compuserve GIF standard was developed by Compuserve for its proprietary network. GIFs achieve their small size because they compress the color space of the file to 256 or fewer colors (called indexed color). The proliferation of the Web has seen some interesting developments in the GIF format—primarily the allowance of an alpha channel that can make defined colors within the image transparent, and the addition of multiple-frame GIF animations.

It is important to distinguish the uses of file types. The JPEG and GIF file formats should never be used for images intended to be printed. In order to achieve their small sizes, these formats throw away color information vital to quality reproduction on paper. A consistent problem seen at printing companies today is the submission of Web images for use in printing.

Chapter 10

Image Acquisition and Management

Continuous-tone images, especially color separations, need special consideration in a digital workflow. More than any other type of artwork encountered in high-end printing, these images are consistently larger in size, more sensitive to color- and quality-related decisions, and more prone to error in the production process. Traditionally, the creation of color separations was entirely within the purview of highly skilled professionals. Years of apprenticeship and experience were drawn on by these craftsmen working with costly and complex procedures to produce final printed color that met the requirements of the process.

The situation today in the market of color has radically changed. The proliferation of low-cost devices and desktop computers has put the ability to create color separations in the hands of anyone willing to make a small investment in hardware and software. Overzealous marketing has given the erroneous impression that color reproduction is a commodity gauged only by the quality of the equipment.

Before the advent of desktop scanners, most production workflows were closed-loop systems. This means that input to the system was controlled completely in-house. All color separations were produced by the same company that also printed the final piece. This gave the printer the ability to optimize the separations for specific printing conditions. With the movement of color separations to the creator side of the workflow, most printers are currently working in an open-loop system. Instead of photographic originals being supplied to the printer, scans from a variety of sources are being submitted. Often these images have been created by people with no real understanding of the requirements to achieve good color reproduction.

Managing the flow of images through a printing plant involves more than just making strategic decisions about file management. The quality of images must be assessed in terms of needed resolution at reproduction size, correct color space, and adjustment for specific press and paper conditions. Values related to color reproduction must be measured and passed on to the creators of separations. In an open-loop workflow, it must be decided where accountability lies for color. If scans are being submitted by clients, who is responsible for achieving acceptable results on press?

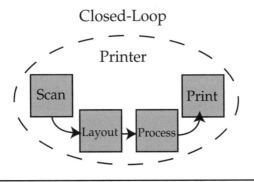

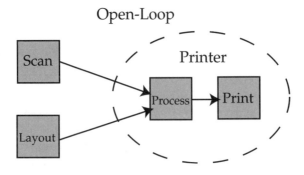

In closed-loop systems, all work is done inside a single company.

Scanner Evolution

The first digital devices to be introduced into the print production workflow were scanners in the 1970s. These scanners did not have the benefit of sophisticated computer controls that we see on scanners today. Rather, they relied on a set of analog controls to manipulate the flow of voltage representing the image data. Instead of creating a digital file, the scanner was directly connected to a film recorder that imaged loose four-color separations. Though this seems inefficient in comparison to today's software-driven scanners, in the context of the technology available at the time, these scanners were in fact state-of-the-art pieces of equipment that required an enormous set of skills to operate.

It is important to avoid confusing the quality of the internal separation-creating components of scanners with the control interface. Ultimately, a scanner is only as good as its capability to capture the image, and these scanners can (and are) still used today to produce some of the highest quality reproductions available.

As proprietary Color Electronic Prepress Systems (CEPS) were introduced in the 1980s, it was recognized that instead of imaging directly to film, it would be helpful if the image could be saved digitally. The file could then be electronically edited for color and placed in position on a page. Original high-end scanners were retrofitted so they could produce a digital file rather than being imaged directly to film.

When the desktop publishing revolution occurred in the late 1980s, scanners were needed that were small and affordable enough to be attached to personal computers. Early high-end scanners were large enough to fill a small room and could cost up to a half-million dollars—well out of the reach of most creative firms. By the early 1990s, imaging technology had advanced to the point that desktop scanners became a reality. Though the first few generations of desktop scanners had severe quality and resolution limitations, within several years devices were available that were technically capable of producing adequate separations.

Today, desktop scanners are available in a wide variety of formats ranging in price from less than 50 dollars to more than 50,000 dollars. Digital cameras are also being integrated as sources for image input.

Defining Scanner Characteristics
Despite the wide variety of prices and formats that are available in the desktop scanner market, there are a few characteristics that can be used to define any scanner. These provide a way to quantitatively compare different devices to each other when making a purchase or use decision.

Every scanner has a maximum resolution associated with it. Scanner resolution is properly measured in samples per inch, a sample being the smallest piece of pixel data the scanner is capable of reading. There are two distinct types of resolution: optical and interpolated. Optical resolution is the physical resolution of the device and the most important measurement. Optical resolution is the real resolution of the scanner. Interpolated resolution is the maximum resolution the scanner software can generate out of the optical resolution. Because in interpolation the software is creating pixel data based on the values of surrounding pixels, any decision should be based on the optical resolution, not the interpolated resolution.

Scanners are also differentiated by dynamic range. Generally, dynamic range is a measure of the density range a scanner is capable of seeing. As a frame of reference, reflective originals normally have a maximum density of around 2.0, whereas transmissive originals have a maximum density approaching 4.0. A higher dynamic range in a scanner represents the ability of that device to differentiate tones in the darker areas. If you are trying to scan 35mm slides with a scanner that has a dynamic range of only 2.5, then any of the shadow tones above 2.5 will be seen by the scanner as flat black. The same scanner, however, could be used for most reflective work without problems.

Newer scanners are available that can create images with high bit-depths. The bit-depth represents the number of different tones that can be represented within a single pixel. Most scanners can achieve 8-bit color, producing 2(8) power (256) tone variations in a single pixel. Some scanners have bit-depths as high as 2(10) or 2(12), called respectively 10-bit or 12-bit depth. Though higher bit-depths can record more data per pixel, images usually have to be converted back to 8-bit color before they can be imaged.

When comparing scanners, all three measurements must be assessed. A scanner that has a bit-depth of 12 but a dynamic range of 1.5 is professionally useless. Likewise, a scanner with a dynamic range of 3.0 but optical resolution of only 150 samples per inch is equally useless for print applications.

Photomultiplier Tube Scanners
The best available scanners are based on photomultiplier tubes (PMTs). A PMT works similar to a television or computer monitor, except that instead of converting electrical energy to light, a PMT converts light to electrical energy. Because PMTs are very sensitive to light, they have high dynamic ranges. With PMT scanners, originals are typically mounted to a clear plastic drum that rotates across a light source and optical aperture; thus these devices are often called drum scanners. By controlling the speed of the drum and the size of the aperture, very high resolutions—up to 12,000 samples per inch—can be achieved.

Most professional-level scanners are PMT based. They are typically much higher in price than other types of scanners but are capable of producing the very best reproductions.

Charge-Coupled Device Scanners
Most desktop scanners, and all flatbed scanners, use a light-sensitive charge-coupled device (CCD) to convert light to electrical energy. CCD scanners are the most inexpensive scanners available but have commensurate limitations compared to PMT scanners. CCD devices are limited in their resolutions to 1,200 samples per inch. CCD devices typically also have lower dynamic ranges than PMT scanners, though there are some CCD models available that can exceed dynamic ranges of 3.5. The resolution of CCD scanners is determined in two directions. One direction is the limit of the chip itself. The other axis is determined by the motor that steps the CCD across the image. Thus, CCD scanners often will have resolutions like 600x1,200 or 300x600. Digital cameras also use CCDs to record an image through a set of filters.

Copy-Dot Scanners

A relatively new type of scanner available today is a copy-dot scanner. These devices have been developed as a direct result of computer-to-plate workflows. As a company moves into computer-to-plate, it must have some way of converting existing film separations into digital files. A copy-dot scanner reads four pieces of separation films in register, and then saves a single file that can be placed into an electronic document for imaging. Copy-dot scanners are a requirement for a company moving to computer-to-plate that has existing film archives or customers that still send in film instead of digital files.

Fundamentals of Color Reproduction

A scanner does not operate in a vacuum. It is an input device that needs to be characterized according to the output of the system. The biggest problem with desktop scanning in an open-loop production system is a lack of understanding by an inexperienced scanner operator of the basic issues of color reproduction. Most of the work to characterize a scanner is actually done by characterizing the output of the system within which the scanner functions. Characterizing the input for the scanner can be achieved only when we have established values for a specific printing condition. Images destined for a digital printer must be created differently than images destined for lithography or any other process.

Though this may seem enormously basic, it is the foremost area of problems today in creating color separations. The minimum tests necessary to characterize the process are highlight dot, shadow dot, midtone, tone-value increase (dot gain), gray balance, color correction, and black generation. The only way to generate this data is to run a test form using the exact ink set/substrate combination we wish to profile. There is no shortcut for this process.

The highlight and shadow-dot tests establish the upper and lower reproduction limits of the system. The lower limit represents the lightest dot that can be held on the system we are characterizing. Anything below this value will be blown out. The higher limit represents the largest dot we can print without plugging, or filling in, the spaces between halftone dots. Anything above this limit will fill to solid. These establish the physical endpoints of the printing system. Printing patches of the process colors in ascending order from 1% to 15% and from 85% to 100% in 1% increments allows us to verify these end points. A visual evaluation of this test is sufficient to provide the needed data.

The midtone test lets us determine how much dot gain our system has. Dot gain is the increase in size of a printing dot from film to press sheet. It is caused by plate exposure, pressure within the press, and absorption of ink by the substrate. By using the Murray-Davies formula, we can determine from the solid ink patch, tint ink patch, and known input exactly how much gain the system produces. The value we are most interested in is the output of a 50% dot input, since this is roughly the area of highest dot gain.

A gray balance test establishes the correct combination of process inks by percentage needed to achieve neutral values. This test is necessary because all process inks have some impurities, which we refer to as contamination or hue error. Not only are all process inks contaminated, but different types, brands, and even batches of process inks have different levels of contaminants. Gray balance tests should not be assessed visually. Rather, the patches should be measured by a colorimeter for a*b* values that are closest to those of the substrate. Gray balance needs to be established for at least three areas: highlights, midtone, and shadows.

Another test needed because of the hue error inherent in process color inks is for color correction. This gives us proper values for the two-color overprints red, green, and blue. This test is better assessed using a densitometer to measure for the highest hue error values than to attempt a visual determination of the "best" overprint colors. The data generated from this test gives us a base to begin from when we later need to characterize the input combination of scanner light source with photographic dyes, as well as in making editorial color changes to separations.

The final basic test we need to make is to determine the black-generation settings for the system. Black generation allows us to control the total amount of ink on the paper and comes in two flavors: UCR or GCR. The main number we want to determine is the total area coverage (TAC). The TAC represents a percentage up to

400, given that printing 100% of all four process colors would give us the maximum value. There are a number of published standards that specify the TAC for a system, such as SWOP, SNAP or GRACoL. To provide consistency, it is normally recommended that printers use the appropriate standards for their systems.

Though a full discussion of print characteristics is beyond the scope of this book, be advised that these minimum values are absolutely necessary to get predictable color results from scanned images. A printer should be able to provide all of these specifications on request. Always get and apply these values before preparing color separations for printing.

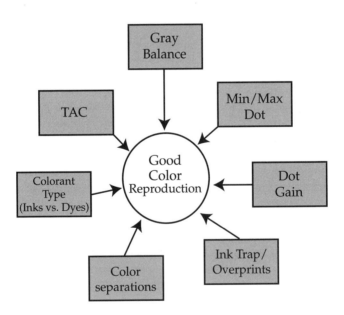

Good color reproduction results from accounting for many variables.

Adjusting Scans for Different Original Types
When we scan a color image, there are several variables that need to be taken into account. Physically, the scanner generates light from some source; that light passes through or is reflected from the original; the light then passes through either a red, green, or blue filter and is converted into an electrical signal using either a charge-coupled device (CCD) or a photomultiplier tube (PMT). That electrical signal can then be used to create a digital record, or file, of the image, or sent directly to a film recorder for imaging. There are two variables, then, to account for: light source and colorant of the original.

Understanding why we need to characterize for these input variables requires some explanation of the mathematics of color. In an overly simplified model, a light source has a certain range of radiative emissions over the visible spectrum. Some scanner light sources will tend to be more blue or more red because of this distribution. With the same idea, colorants absorb different distributions of light over the visual spectrum. Color then can be defined as a function involving the integration of the product of the spectral power curve (light source) with the spectral reflectance curve (colorant) over the range of the visual spectrum.

Another problematic issue is a variation in the absorption properties of colorants. No two colorants have exactly the same spectral reflectance curve. This means that a red in a Fuji chrome has different color than the red in a Kodak chrome. There is also a difference between colorants in transmissive versus reflective originals—the red in a Kodak chrome is different than the red in a Kodak print.

Occasionally, changing scanner settings for different originals is referred to as "adjusting how the scanner sees color." This is a little too vague a definition to be useful. A better way of considering it is that we are adjusting for the relationship between the photographic dyes in the original and the specific color properties of the scanner light source. What it means is that for each type of original, categorized by the type of colorant, we need a separate set of scanner settings. And because of PMT sensitivity changes over time, we must also keep the settings updated.

The combination of different originals and different printing processes provides a nearly limitless number of permutations, which each needs its own characterizations. This is the heart, and the difficulty, of the correct scanning process. Using the settings for reproducing a Fuji chrome original on coated paper to reproduce a Kodak chrome with laser-safe inks on uncoated paper will produce only garbage. This is the reason why, even today, many professional designers still rely on their printers to produce high-quality color separations.

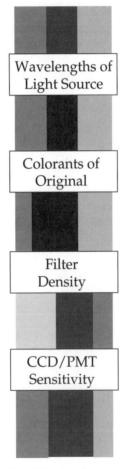

Scanners must be calibrated for different originals and inherent problems.

Color-Management Software

In 1995 the International Color Consortium (ICC) was founded with the goal of setting standards for creating color-management profiles that would allow some level of automation in the process of color reproduction. Color management takes advantage of the processing power of computers to treat color reproduction as a mathematical rather than subjective process. The idea behind color-management software is fairly easy to understand, though its implementation is much more difficult to accomplish.

At the center of ICC-based color management is the idea of profiling the three main devices used for color reproduction: scanners, monitors, and output devices. By characterizing these devices to known values, a mathematical transformation matrix can be set up within which color in an image can be optimized for reproduction on a different device using CIE L*a*b* as its transformation space. The process of characterizing a scanner using ICC is straightforward.: An IT8.7/1 (transmissive) or IT8.7/2 (reflective) target of the appropriate film or paper type is scanned using basic settings.

Notice that this takes into account the base problem of characterizing scanner input relative to colorant type. The resultant RGB scan is then imported into a specialized software package that has built into it a data set for the exact values of each patch. By comparing the scanned values to the known values, a profile is generated that characterizes the reproduction capabilities of the scanner. This, of course, does us no good unless all of the devices in the workflow are profiled.

A monitor profile is generated again by software that takes into account the phosphors, gamma, white point, and black point of the unit. To generate a printer profile, a target with known values is printed on the final device—whether that be a lithographic press or home inkjet printer—and then, much like the scanner profile, read into a software package that compares the output generated to the input values.

Of particular importance to the creation of the printer profile is that it does take into account the six critical areas of characterization mentioned earlier.

To put it all together, the scanner generates RGB data, which is then tagged with a profile that contains a matrix for transforming the RGB data into L*a*b* according to the characteristics from the known IT8.7/1 (or /2) target. The image, now in L*a*b*, which is known as the profile connection space (PCS), will be converted to the format specified for the destination profile (either monitor or printer), according to the matrix that was created when the data was imported from the printed target.

The image is then optimized for reproduction on the selected printer. Note that nowhere do we make the claim that we will get an exact match from device to device. This is a widely held misconception about color management. Color management serves only to optimize the file for the device.

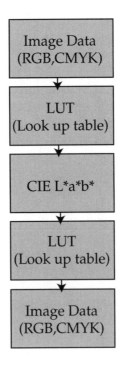

*Color management uses a simple transformation through CIE L*a*b*.*

ICC Problems

Though the ICC approach to characterization and color control seems to work well, it is not without its limitations. ICC color management is still image oriented. Though this is acceptable if we consider only color separations, in the printing industry we generally print pages and pieces, not just images. Extending that concept, what we really put on a plate is an imposition—a collection of pages. Until color management can address characterization at the form level, it has limited usefulness within a production workflow.

A second issue, which does have serious ramifications for the area of color separations, is in the control of the black printer in CMYK to CMYK transformations. Generally we want firm control over the choice of GCR/UCR and the corresponding TAC.

If we consider the scenario of digital proofers, a prime candidate for the use of color management, what we would like to have happen is to take a file that has been separated for press and have color management force a conversion for a match on the proofer. In reality, what occurs is that the CMYK file is converted to L*a*b* PCS and then reconverted back to CMYK with different black-generation specifications. The original black printer has been destroyed with no way to recover it. This is completely unacceptable for controlling the reproduction of color separations. The only way around this is to keep the file in RGB and make the transformation to CMYK twice—once for the press and once for the proofer.

A third problem with the ICC approach has to do with the availability and compatibility of associated software. Though the latest version of ColorSync (color management for Macintosh) runs at the operating system level, an application must have been designed to access it—called ColorSync-savvy. At this time there are few applications that are ColorSync-savvy, and those that are do not always give identical results (QuarkXPress vs. PageMaker, for example). There is also an issue of compatibility across operating systems. Color management for Microsoft Windows, called ICM2, cannot guarantee a match to the results generated by ColorSync.

A fourth problem with color management is that the correct reproduction of color separations requires a knowledge of the entire reproduction process. No two images are exactly alike, and very few reproduction processes share exactly the same characteristics. Ultimately, the correct reproduction of an image requires a trained operator to make the correct choice—an intelligence level even our fastest computers are far from attaining.

Although ICC color management cannot be considered a current panacea for all workflow and image reproduction problems, there are opportunities where color-managed files can be extremely useful. Digital proofing is one such position in the workflow. The difficulty is in maintaining a consistent source profile and color space.

Color management is still a young technology. Despite PostScript's initial problems, when released it ended up changing the industry. It seems likely that ultimately color management will have a similar effect.

Image Management and OPI
The large sizes of images require a strategy for managing the flow of image files through a company. Copying these files across networks or even using removable disks can cause huge time delays in a workflow. Processing these files on workstations can create further delays. The intent is to limit the number of transmissions needed for these files by providing a structure based on centralized location—an image server, along with software that helps to automate control of the files.

Open Prepress Interface (OPI) is an effective tool that can be used to reduce the network and processing burden created by large image files. In an OPI workflow, high-resolution images are placed on a centralized image server, which automatically creates a low-resolution copy of the image.

The low-res file is placed into the page layout and cropped or sized as needed. When the page-layout file is printed, a marker called an OPI tag is associated with the low-res file. When the RIP sees the OPI tag, it automatically swaps the low-res copy for the high-res original. The result is an automated system that limits network transfer and moves the bulk of the processing time to the RIP rather than the workstation.

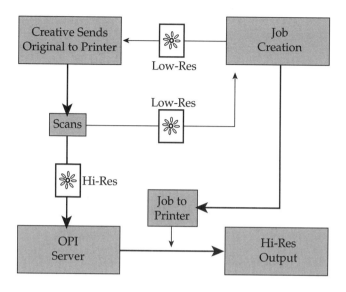

An OPI workflow is one example in which production involves the designer.

Though desktop scanners are widely available today, many images call for a quality or enlargement that can only be provided by using a high-end PMT drum scanner. Because most of this equipment is generally owned by the printer, many design firms still send in photographic originals to be scanned by the printer. This is one of the most useful instances for initiating an OPI strategy.

After scanning the image, the printer merely copies the high-resolution file onto its image server and returns the low-resolution copy to the designer to be placed. In this example, the high-resolution image only needs a single network transfer: from scanner to image server. This saves the printing and design companies the time and expense of handling and processing large files.

In any high-end printing environment, a color image must be in CMYK to reproduce properly. Traditionally, all images were converted to CMYK immediately upon scanning them, because that was ultimately how they would have to end up anyway. But the new environment of graphic communications is forcing some changes in this workflow. Documents often are repurposed from print into Internet or multimedia work. Images may need to be printed traditionally but also used for some digital printing applications. Because a single image may go through a number of different cycles, there is a trend toward keeping images in RGB until the point at which they are imaged by a particular device.

RGB images have a number of advantages over CMYK images. Because there are only three color channels in RGB images, they are 25% smaller in size. The RGB color space is also much larger than the CMYK color space—converting to CMYK loses much of the data that was contained in the original RGB format. By keeping an image in RGB, it is possible to optimize a single image for multiple uses.

Support for RGB workflows is coming from several different directions. Many RIP manufacturers are including the option for in-RIP separations, allowing the RIP to automatically convert from RGB to CMYK. ICC color management is geared directly toward a pure RGB workflow, allowing images to be converted to CMYK with specialized look-up tables for each device. Major graphic arts page-layout applications have also provided support for RGB-to-CMYK conversion without the need to use a dedicated image-editing program.

RGB workflow shows much promise in allowing the industry to adapt to changing demands, but it has not been widely adapted. This is directly attributable to a lack of trust from printers in allowing their software to make color-critical decisions for them. As color-management and in-RIP automation technologies mature, and more companies gain experience and confidence in working with RGB, it is likely that in the near future the majority of images moving through the print production workflow will be in the RGB format.

Chapter 11

Proofing in the Graphic Arts

At its most basic, a proof is a sample that represents the status of a job at a given time. Proofs can range from simply viewing a document on a computer monitor, called "soft proofing," all the way to final color proofs that represent a legally binding contract between printer and customer. Most jobs go through a number of different levels of proof, beginning with word-processed copy.

Proofing gives accountability and verification to the production process. It allows the printer and the customer to be certain that the job is produced according to the desired specifications and quality level. Before computer-to-plate production, off-press proofs were exposed directly from the film that was used to create the plates. Prepress or off-press proofing is actually a relatively recent development. Until the 1960s, it was not uncommon for proofing to take place at the press when the job was run, or to be proofed with an initial special print run.

Film-based off-press proofing was first used in the creation of maps by the United States government in the 1950s and did not become commercially viable until the DuPont Cromalin was released in 1971. Since then, film-based off press proofing has been the standard for predicting the results of a press run.

In 1985, the introduction of the Macintosh computer—followed shortly thereafter by software that could compose a full page and the development of the PostScript page-description language—

changed the basic method for producing printed work. What began simply has developed into an entirely new paradigm for print manufacturing, culminating in computer-to-plate (CTP) and digital workflows. This move to CTP—the removal of film from the workflow—is the driving force behind the current changes in off-press proofing.

With the possibility now to maintain all work in the digital domain, the problems inherent in film-based proofing are becoming part of the motivation to leave film behind. One of the biggest problems of film-based proofs is simply the fact that film is required to create them. In a digital workflow, this is an unnecessary and wasteful step.

The removal of film from the workflow means that proofs must now be generated directly from digital files. These proofs must still retain all of the reliability that printers and clients are accustomed to receiving from their traditional film-based proofs.

The Proofing Cycle

People who are new to printing, whether designers or in-plant, often find the most confusing aspect of the business to be the proofing cycle. Jobs follow specific levels of proofs that create increasing levels of verification. It is important to understand exactly what can be expected from a particular type of proof and what should be looked for in each proof.

Any proof can generally be placed into one of three categories: preliminary proof, content or positional proof, and contract color proof. Each of these categories has a relative increase in the demands that are placed on it by printer and client in terms of the proof's ability to act as a predictor of final press output.

The preliminary proof is normally used to judge the progress of a job, without acting as a perfect predictor of the press, and can be used to judge color or the position of elements on a page. Quality levels for preliminary proofing need only be good enough to show the basic look of the work in progress. Preliminary proofs for position are as simple as a set of laser prints showing where elements are located or separated by color breaks.

Color preliminary proofs generally need only be visually acceptable. Individual preliminary color proofs are often made directly after scanning a color separation so that any errors can be caught before the job continues through the production workflow. These loose proofs are called scatter, random, or float proofs, depending on what area of the world you're in.

A final content or positional proof is used to show positioning and final layout. Because content proofs are used only to verify correct position, they need to be exact in size but can have some variation in color. Often these proofs are used to show the position of all pages on the final imposition.

Traditionally, dylux (blueline) proofs made directly from the stripped film flats were used to proof content. By varying the exposure for different colors, trapping and correct color breaks could be verified by the client and printer.

Digital workflows allow many more options for content proofing because RIPed files can be viewed on a computer monitor or imaged directly to paper. A content proof becomes extremely important at the late stages of the workflow, after any author alterations have been made to the copy.

The most important category of proof to the printing industry is the contract proof. Once signed by the client, it becomes a legally binding document requiring the printer to match all elements, position, and color before payment will be made by the client. A contract proof is judged by its ability to match the press output in resolution, colorants, tone reproduction, and substrate. In contrast to a preliminary proof, the contract proof must be verifiable through either densitometric or colorimetric measurements.

The enormous demand placed on contract proofs means that these devices are usually very expensive and require constant calibration and maintenance. Once a contract proof has been signed, it will be given to the press operator to be used as a guide for matching the color in the job. Thus, the value of any contract proofing device is ultimately in its ability to match a standard press sheet.

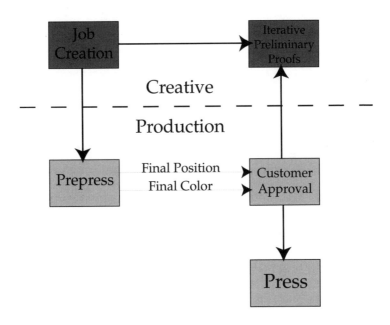

A single job is proofed many times throughout the design and production process.

Traditional Proofs

Traditional proofs are characterized by being exposed from the same film that will be used to create the plates. Though a digital workflow requires digital proofing, it is still important to understand the basics of traditional proofs. A blueline (also called a dylux) is a proof generated by exposing a special paper with the same film that will be used to create the plates for the press. Different colors are expressed by varying exposures to create different shades of blue and should be marked by the person who creates the proof, called "color breaking" the proof. This proof should be an exact match to the final job—including any finishing. Bluelines are inexpensive and extremely accurate proofs, excellent for checking copy, trim, bleeds, folds, and register. In general, you should request a blueline for any job that is being printed with conventional offset lithography. If your job has folds, a blueline is the only way you can check their accuracy.

Laminate proofs, like bluelines, are created from the same films that will be used to create the printing plates. An individual donor sheet for each process color is exposed and then laminated onto a receiver sheet or final substrate. Laminate proofs are capable of producing an extremely accurate representation of process (CMYK) colors. Imation MatchPrint and Fuji ColorArt are two of the most popular forms of laminate proofs. If a job uses process color, you should request a laminate proof and carefully check it to be certain that the colors in the proof match your specifications. Most complex jobs require both a color laminate and blueline proof. Use the laminate to check and approve the color and the blueline to check and approve position and geometry.

Digital Proofs
The use of computer-to-plate in a digital workflow requires the use of a digital proofer, because film is no longer being created. Though digital proofers have long been used for preliminary proofs, the challenge for digital proofers is ultimately their reliability and acceptance as contract proofers. The time-tested success of analog, film-based proofs has hampered the acceptance of digital proofs by clients. Nonetheless, the adoption of computer-to-plate means that contract proofing must fall into the scope of digital proofers.

One major reason cited for clients' not wishing to accept digital proofs seems to be simple human reticence to change. There is a comfort level associated with analog proofs that is simply not established for digital proofs. Another problem clients seem to have with digital proofs is that many of these devices produce continuous-tone images rather than the reassuring halftone dots they have come to expect from high-quality proofs.

Surprisingly, this seems to go against the opinion of most experts in this field: that digital proofs are capable of far better results than analog proofs. Digital proofs produce stable and repeatable color at great cost savings. Analog proofs are often limited in the variety of substrates that can be used for imaging and, because they are based on exposure, are difficult to calibrate to a specific printing condition. Digital proofs can take advantage of the flexibility of a digital file and the computational speed of computers with color-matching systems to provide a color match for almost any printing condition.

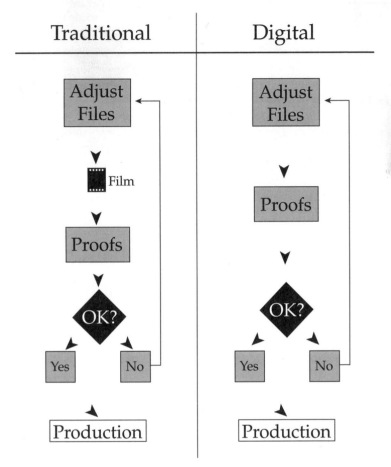

Digital proofing removes expensive and time-consuming film generation.

What seems to be at issue in the controversy between analog and digital proofs is a conceptualization of the purpose of the proof. Until very recently, color matching in a contract proof was based on matching exact density, dot gain and gray balance. These items, however, can more properly be termed as process-control issues rather than color-matching issues. The attempt with a proof is to match color, not dots. The use of colorimetry, whether through some proprietary standard or International Color Consortium (ICC) standard, is both a requirement and advantage in achieving color matching with digital proofing devices.

The practical unreliability of integrating current color-management systems technology today contributes to the difficulty of viewing proofing as a process. Perceptually, it can be seen by the client and printer as attempting to support one untested technology—digital proofing—with another untested technology: color management. Combining the flexibility and power possible through maintaining the job digitally throughout the workflow creates new opportunities in proofing that were outside the bounds of reality in traditional analog workflows. This creates chances to reduce costs and cycle time in the production workflow.

Dye-Sublimation and Thermal-Wax Proofers

Dye-sublimation (more properly called dye-diffusion) and thermal-wax devices are the most popular devices on the market for digital color proofers. The two devices are grouped together because they basically work the same, except in the choice of a dye or wax-based colorant. Many devices are sold with the capability to handle either type of donor sheet. In these devices, a donor sheet with one of the process colors is drawn across the paper. A print head then moves across the donor sheet, applying heat wherever colorant is required. The heat moves the colorant from the donor sheet to the paper. The process is repeated for each color. All of these devices make excellent preliminary color proofers and, with calibration utilities, can be used as contract color proofers for some applications.

Toner Proofers

Toner-based machines are another popular process for color proofing. Similar to photocopiers, they use plastic-based colorants that are applied to the paper by varying an electrostatic charge between the paper and the image carrier. The paper is then heated, which fixes the toner to the paper. Toner-based devices are generally inadequate for contract color proofing because of resolution restrictions that come from the relatively large size of the toner particles, but they are widely used as inexpensive and reliable preliminary color and position proofers. Toner-based machines are having the most impact on the industry in their use as digital presses. Xeikon and Indigo, as well as Canon and Xerox, are producing popular toner-based digital presses. Because each impression can be completely different, there are important applications for toner-based printing in the areas of personalization and short-run color work.

Inkjet Proofers

Inkjet proofers are by far the most popular color proofers available today. They range from household printers as inexpensive as $100 to professional-level proofers that can image an entire form at one time and cost well over $20,000. Though there are several different categories of inkjet technology, essentially they all work by ejecting drops of process color dyes onto a sheet of paper. Inkjet proofers are enormously popular because they combine the ability to create contract color–level proofing with a relatively inexpensive price. The Scitex IRIS proofer is one of the most-used inkjet printers in production environments.

Halftone Digital Proofers

The choice of whether to use a halftone or continuous-tone digital proofer is the most divided issue in the realm of digital proofing. Halftone digital proofers are defined as those devices that image using traditional halftone-dot structures. Some of the more popular examples are the Kodak Approval, Polaroid PolaProof, Presstek hdqp, and Creo Spectrum. The latter two use the same marking engine to image both proofs and plates, a relatively new development in digital proofing technology.

Continuous-tone proofers make up the bulk of digital proofing options, but because they lack halftone dots they are often condemned as inadequate to the demands of contract proofers. The industry seems to be equally divided as to which is better. For some, the inherent higher resolution and thus ability to accurately render type and line work is cited as the reason for preferring halftone proofers. For others, the issue is more in ability to render color than to exactly match dots, and due to their lower cost they prefer continuous-tone devices.

Price is one obviously differentiating factor in the choice of proofer. Effective inkjet production proofers can be purchased for as low as $10,000, whereas halftone proofers are normally more than $100,000. Ultimately, the most important factor in making the choice of proofer type is the client's willingness to accept the proof as contract quality. Some companies claim that their largest clients simply will not accept for contract purposes a proof that lacks halftone dots. Reasons include reliability for showing dot-related problems like moiré, and a concern that there will be a color shift between continuous-tone and halftone printing.

There is some suggestion that the difficulty with clients' accepting continuous-tone proofs derives solely from a lack of desire to change rather than any inherent deficiency in the device. Continuous-tone proofs often are wrongly evaluated against a halftone proof of the same image rather than against the final press sheet. This suggests that there is a learning curve involved with the interpretation of continuous-tone proofs. Success in achieving client acceptance of continuous-tone proofs has been related to moving slowly into the process so that the client has time to develop comfort with the results of continuous-tone proofs.

Many experts believe that the inkjet and dye-diffusion processes most associated with continuous-tone devices actually lend themselves to better color-matching capabilities than halftone devices. The ability of these devices, especially inkjets, to modulate the amount of colorant placed on the proofing substrate allows color management to more effectively simulate any printing process. Continuous-tone proofers suffer more from a perception of inadequacy rather than an actual inadequacy.

Soft Proofing
"Soft proofing" is defined as the use of a CRT monitor to preview how a job will look on press. The advantages to using soft proofing are that it is accessible and established, most people already have monitors, and it is inexpensive, requiring no consumables. In a sense, soft proofs are used every day to preview images as they are scanned or pages as they are laid out. Given the obvious advantages, many people have suggested that soft proofing will eventually become a viable technology.

The controversy over the use of soft proofing is in the area of contract proofing. A number of reasons have been stated for the unacceptability of soft proofing as a contract proof. Monitors are based on additive color theory, whereas printing is based on subtractive color theory. The phosphors in CRT monitors are inherently unstable and prone to drifting over time. And maintaining correct viewing conditions becomes difficult if not impossible.

Technology advancements may offer some help in the area of accepting soft proofs as contract proofs. Some experts say that advancement in color-management technology, particularly the ICC standards, will create better results in CRT proofing. If soft proofing is unacceptable as a contract proof, that does not automatically exclude it from having value as some other type of proof. The ultimate value of soft proofing may be as a content rather than contract proof. The Committee for Graphic Arts Technology Standards (CGATS) is currently working on approving a standardized format for Adobe's Portable Document Format (PDF).

The new format, known as PDF/X or PDF Exchange, will require repairs for many of the problems printers have had in using the PDF files for high-end production work. As CGATS makes its decision regarding the acceptance of the PDF/X-1 file format as a standard for exchange, this may well be a successful alternative use for soft proofing.

Remote Proofing
Remote proofing is defined as a situation in which a digital proofer with acceptable quality is maintained on the client site. Images and pages are sent through a network transmission from the printer and then imaged at the client's site. Issues in remote proofing include telecommunications, equipment purchase and maintenance costs, and verification that the system can be maintained in a calibrated state to the appropriate printing system.

In contrast to soft proofing, there seems to be no doubt that the basic enabling technology of available and high-quality devices exists. There are a number of medium-cost, high-quality printing systems available that can be used for successful remote-proofing applications. In fact, many advertising and graphic design agencies have already purchased inkjet systems like the IRIS and Epson 5000 digital proofers for their own internal use.

Telecommunications is a major area of concern for remote proofing. There must be some digital infrastructure in place to allow the transmission of files from printer to client. This is a far from trivial issue. The technology available for high-speed file transfer is not standardized; options range from using ISDN lines to installing Internet T1 trunk lines. Hiring outside companies to manage the infrastructure, like WHAM!NET's WHAM!PROOF, may ease a printer's transition into high-speed telecommunications. Concerns with a client's management information system department, which may not be used to the relatively large sizes of graphics files, need to be addressed up front. Often the internal networks of large companies are based on the ability to handle many transmissions of small files rather than few transmissions of large files.

Verification and maintenance are other issues of remote proofing. There must be a method in place to assure that calibration is maintained at the client site. Likewise, the system must be easy enough to use so that the client feels comfortable with basic calibration and maintenance tasks. There are systems available, however, that allow not only remote verification of calibration but also the tagging of graphics files with the current state of calibration so that both sides of the transfer can be certain that they are seeing the same image.

Another critical issue of remote printing is the cost of the initial device, training, consumables, and the maintenance of the telecommunications link. Who pays for the equipment—the printer or the client? Who maintains the equipment? These decisions are based entirely on the relationship that the printer has with the client. The questions must be handled individually for each client.

Despite these obstacles, remote proofing is attractive to printer as well as client because of its reduction in latency and cycle time. Latency is any time in the workflow in which a job is not being worked on. Often this time is made up of the two-day window in which a proof is being overnighted to and from a client for approval. Even if proofs are generated at the client site and then must be shipped back to the printer, latency and cycle time can still be cut in half.

Special Cases in Proofing
There are some special cases that are particularly problematic for proofing, whether by digital or traditional means. Spot colors are often used in printing but are difficult to proof exactly. For analog laminates, covering the total number of possibilities would require

the printer to inventory thousands of different colorants—an economically unfeasible proposition. Digital proofers typically convert all colors used to process colors. Though this can give an approximation of the special color, many spot colors are unreproducible with process-color equivalents. Despite this problem, most spot colors are proofed using a few special colors that the printer maintains on hand if needed. This, in combination with ink drawdowns and color chips, has worked well for proofing spot and special colors.

New printing techniques such as hi-fi color or frequency modulation (FM) screening also cause problems with proofing. Hi-fi, which uses additional process colors beyond the normal CMYK, requires a special set of colorants to proof and is impossible to proof using current process-color digital proofers. FM screening uses very small dots that create special problems in adjusting for dot gain and other tone-reproduction critical areas.

Often the inability to proof FM-screened images comes from aging equipment that simply lacks the physical ability to resolve dots only 30 or 40 microns in size. Continuous-tone digital proofers, with their ability to tightly control calibration to a specific printing condition, are excellent choices for proofing FM-screened work, assuming that continuous-tone proofs are acceptable to the client. Special cases like these need to be addressed with the printer or service bureau before the job is created, so that alternative proofing methods can be established.

Chapter 12

Raster Image Processor

An imagesetter is essentially only a device that combines a laser with some transport mechanism for moving materials through the machine. The raster image processor, or RIP, is the part of any imaging device that provides the ability to tell the laser exactly where to image the materials. The RIP is just as, if not more, important than the imagesetter. Basically the RIP is responsible for interpreting incoming files, usually PostScript code, and converting them to information that controls how and where the laser will image film, plates, or proofing materials.

Advancements in workflow systems, however, have made the RIP much more powerful, giving it the ability to automate and consolidate multiple tasks within a digital workflow. Any printer that accepts a page-description language must have some type of RIP attached to it. Even home laser printers have RIPs within the device.

The first RIPs were called hardware RIPs. They were proprietary systems that had the interpretation software hard-wired into the machine—basically a dedicated computer. The problem with hardware RIPs is that updating them to a newer version requires purchasing and installing a new card, or even replacing the entire system. With the speed at which computer and RIP technology advances, this quickly becomes a fatal liability and expense.

The next generation of RIPs, called software RIPs, used standard computer platforms—a Macintosh, Windows, or UNIX machine—

with specialized software and networking abilities installed. This gave the advantage of being able to easily upgrade the RIP software as needed, as well as to upgrade to a faster platform as they were available. Software RIPs also provide a measure of redundancy and protection to a workflow. Every job that goes through a shop must travel through the RIP to be imaged. If a hardware RIP goes down (and because they are computers this is inevitable and needs to be planned for), work stops until the RIP can be repaired or replaced. If a software RIP goes down, the RIP can be instantly reinstalled or even moved to a different computer. Virtually all new RIPs sold today are software RIPs.

Many major vendors have now integrated the RIP along with functionality for automating repetitive tasks in the production process, creating a unified workflow/RIP system. Advantages to consolidating functions in the RIP include versatility and centralized control of the process. These RIPs have become far more critical to the workflow than mere printer drivers. Correctly configuring an advanced RIP within the workflow may be the single most important area for improvement of the process.

Regardless of the complexity of an individual type of RIP, all RIP processes can be subdivided into three finite categories. The RIP first interprets the incoming file, usually a PostScript file. Second, the RIP takes the interpreted data and creates an object or display list of individual items within the page. Finally, the RIP applies device-dependent screening and resolution information to the display list, creates a final bitmapped file that can be plotted by the laser, and then streams that data to the imagesetter for imaging.

Interpretation
The first step in the RIP process is to take in and interpret the file that needs to be imaged. For the vast majority of RIPs, this means interpreting PostScript code. There are some exceptions to this. PostScript, though it is the major page-description language in the graphic arts, is not the only page-description language available. Hewlett-Packard's PCL family is one example of a page-description language other than PostScript. Other RIPs are being configured to accept Adobe Acrobat PDF files, but even PDF is related to and derived from PostScript.

PostScript is a high-level programming language. What differentiates it from languages like C++ is that PostScript has been optimized to describe graphic objects, and that PostScript is interpreted rather than compiled. When a program is written in C++, it is compiled into an executable application that can be run by another computer. When you run a program you are not running it from the original program, called the source code. Instead you are running a previously interpreted copy of the program, which is created by compiling the source code.

PostScript is always interpreted from the source code without any intermediate step. The RIP acts much like a compiler, interpreting the PostScript code into another, simpler format. PostScript is also interpreted linearly from the beginning of the code to the end. This leads directly to one of the major limitations of PostScript interpretation: Will two different RIPs always interpret the same PostScript code with the same results?

To illustrate this problem, consider a digital workflow that uses a proofer and an imagesetter, each with its own respective RIP. A PostScript file is generated from a page and then imaged on the proofer. Once the proof has been approved, the same PostScript file is then uploaded to the imagesetter. If the imagesetter's RIP does not interpret the code in the same way as the proofer's RIP, there will be problems in matching the proof to the final piece.

Other problems that can occur in the interpretation stage of the RIP have to do with the way the RIP interprets the PostScript code. The RIP reads the program one line at a time and is unable to skip from place to place within the program. This means that a tremendous amount of redundancy must be included in complex PostScript files so that the RIP is able to have all the information it needs to accurately interpret each step in the code. A single problem near the top of the file means that the entire file is useless. Because PostScript files are so complex, these errors, called PostScript errors, have become a huge problem in the industry.

Object /Display List
Once the RIP has completed interpreting each page, it generates a list of all the objects on that page, along with their placement, called

the display or object list. An object can be a line of type, a box, a rule, or any single item defined with a set of PostScript commands. The object list is a simplified version of the page data that acts as an interim step between the raw PostScript and the application of device-dependent screening and resolution attributes to the page information.

Because the object list is beyond the inconsistencies of PostScript interpretation, there are numerous ways to take advantage of the object list within a workflow. This is the basis for PDF, which is essentially a representation of the object list generated from Post-Script code. Being able to view the object list increases the reliability of the file because there is no chance of error from a reinterpretation of the original PostScript code.

The use of these intermediaries allows RIP Once—Output Many systems to be developed. These systems, called ROOM, interpret an incoming PostScript file and then save the resulting conversion. If further imaging is required, reinterpretation is not necessary. Another similar version of this system is called NORM: Normalize Once—Rasterize Many.

Obviously, if a file has been rasterized it has already had device-dependent characteristics applied to it. ROOM systems get around this limitation by rasterizing the file at the highest needed resolution within the system. For lower-resolution devices, the rasterized file is then acceptable.

Take again our example of a workflow using a proofer and image-setter each with their own RIP, but in this case with the ability of the imagesetter to accept the object list generated from the proofer's RIP. The PostScript file is interpreted by the proofer's RIP, except this time the object list is stored as a separate file before the proofer images the page. If the proof is acceptable, only the object list, not the original PostScript, is uploaded to the imagesetter. Because the file is not reinterpreted, there is a much greater chance that the film will match the proof. This also eliminates potential PostScript errors from the imagesetter's RIP.

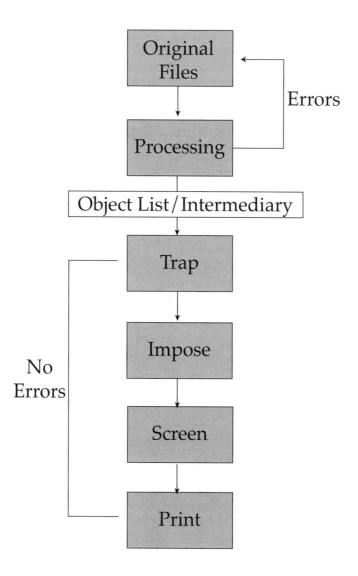

Using an intermediary based on the object list removes most processing errors.

Rasterizing and Streaming
Once a file has been interpreted and an object list generated, the final stage in the process is to apply machine-dependent attributes to the object list and then send the information to the printing device. Because every printing device has different requirements, the result of this process will be different in each case. A raster represents a single line of page data—essentially one pass of the laser across the media. Rasterizing the page, then, is equivalent to breaking the page into the smallest needed sections for the imaging device.

Resolution also must be applied at this stage. The RIP for a 300-DPI laser printer will create a 300-DPI raster file of the page. If the device is a 2,400-DPI imagesetter, the raster file will be at 2,400 DPI. Any rotation to the file is applied at this stage. Screening information, which requires processing the file through a complex algorithm called the threshold matrix, is applied to the file. Finally, the data controlling the laser modulation and media transport is uploaded, or streamed, to the imaging device, and the final page is printed.

It is important to understand that although the object list allows for opportunity to reduce error in the workflow, the same advantage does not exist for rasterized files. A rasterized image has been optimized for reproduction only on a single device, under a single set of circumstances. The raster image for our hypothetical proofer above cannot be reused with the imagesetter. Once the page has been rasterized, it can no longer be sent to a different device.

Spots, Dots, and Pixels
One of the major areas of confusion in referencing different RIPs, images, or devices comes from using the wrong terms to define machine- or image-dependent resolution. When confronted with the wide variety of acronyms that exist in the industry, it is easy to confuse some of the basic resolution-related elements that compose images or printed pages.

The basic building block of a device's resolution is the area exposed by one single point of laser light, called a spot or machine dot. The number of spots that a device images in 1 inch (centimeter everywhere else in the world) represents that machine's resolution, more properly called its addressability. An imagesetter with an address-ability of 2,400 spots per inch (SPI) has the ability to image 2,400 single points of laser light (or thermal energy) in 1 inch.

A dot represents a single halftone dot and is built out of laser spots. The number of halftone dots in an inch is referred to as the screen ruling for a printed image, also sometimes called the line screen, and referenced by the term lines per inch (LPI). The relationship be-tween laser spots and halftone dots establishes the number of tonal variations possible to achieve in an image.

For example, assume we are printing an image at 100 LPI, using a device that has 1,000-SPI addressability. Dividing the addressabili-ty (1,000) by the screen ruling (100) gives us the total number of laser spots—10—that can be assigned to each halftone dot in one dimension. Because we work in a two-dimensional grid, we end up with a square for each halftone dot that measures 10 x 10, or a total of 100 laser spots for each halftone dot.

This means there are 101 different tonal variations that this halftone dot could potentially take (including zero, which would represent paper). Normally it is best to have 256 tonal variations, so in this case we would have to either reduce the screen ruling or increase the addressability of the device.

The number 256 appears often when working with digital files and imaging. The reason is that most color systems work with 8-bit col-or, or 2^8, which equals 256. When we discuss the bit-depth of files, we speak in terms of 1-bit, 8-bit, or 12-bit files. This merely repre-sents the value of 2^x possible tone values. Why pick 8-bit over a higher value? Eight bits just happens to be an old standard for rep-resenting computer data.

In fact, many scanners use 12-bit color depth to record the image. This gives 4,096 tonal variations instead of only 256. The problem, unfortunately, is that most software and imaging systems are un-able to accept 12-bit files. They must be converted back to 8-bit for-mat before being imaged. The use of PostScript 3, which can image in 12-bit for some applications, may change this.

Halftone cells

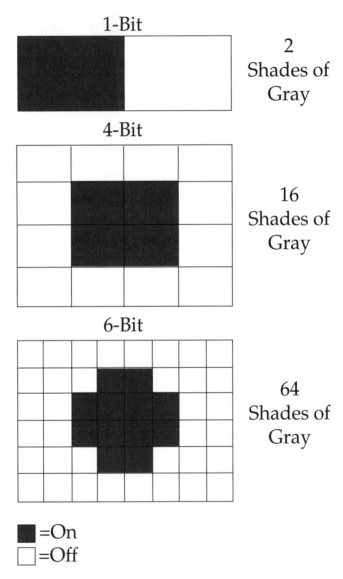

Bit-depth translates directly into tone variations.

The term "pixel" came from picture element and should only be used to reference the resolution of image data. Often an image will be scanned at 300 dots per inch. The correct term for this should be pixels per inch or PPI. Pixels can take multiple attributes depending on the type of art they represent. Pixels can also have tonal variation themselves, which is represented very differently than the tonal variations represented by halftone dots (covered in depth in the chapter on images). Pixel data is used by the RIP to establish which laser spots will be imaged on the plate or film, thus creating halftone dots.

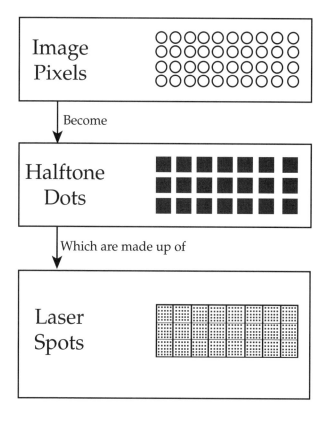

Halftone dots are created from laser spots, which are controlled by pixel values.

Though it is important to be aware of the proper use for these terms, in reality we usually have to look at the context of these terms to define them. When a laser printer is advertised at 600 dots per inch, we know (or have to assume) that what the ad really means is that the laser printer has an addressability of 600 spots per inch. A scanned image at 300 dots per inch is really at 300 pixels per inch. Understanding the relationship between spots, dots, and pixels will allow you to logically identify these attributes no matter which term is used.

Separating the RIPing Process
The first RIPs were single boxes that processed all three steps—interpretation, object list, and screening—consecutively without interruption. Because each of these steps is independent, significant efficiency and opportunities can be gained from dividing the steps into their basic components. PDF is the most overt change to the industry as a result of this separation of processes. A PDF is similar to a viewable object list file.

By having a RIP generate PDF files, it is possible to implement a proofing procedure that allows interpreted PDF files to be transmitted across networks and used for proofing on a computer monitor. Though this is generally inadequate for color proofing, it is an excellent option for proofing the position of elements and type on a page. Using PDF or other intermediate object list proofing can often take days off the production cycle of a job.

Some companies have approached the separation of the RIPing process by using different computers for each step. Memory-intensive operations such as interpretation and screening can be performed on a processor independent of any other function. This helps to add speed in processing files, while still controlling the workflow by avoiding adding additional RIPs. These systems allow multiple processors to be added as needed.

A related concept that is gaining popularity is RIP Once—Output Many (ROOM) and Normalize Once—Rasterize Many (NORM) systems. These systems, which are normally based on imaging entire forms rather than single pages, take advantage of the flexibility of object lists by performing the memory-intensive operations involved with processing files only once. The resulting files may be redistributed to other devices without the need for reprocessing.

This allows the same file to be used on a proofer and then redirected to an imagesetter or digital press without having to open and print the file from a workstation. Though ROOM and NORM systems seem promising, many printers have found limited value in these systems, because if changes are required to a job, no matter how small, it must be reprinted anyway—and few jobs manage to make it through the process without some customer changes.

The single-page variant of ROOM and NORM systems, known as late-binding systems, shows much more promise to be useful in the industry. Individual pages are RIPed and then saved onto a hard disk. Rather than imposing the pages before sending them to the RIP, the RIPed and saved pages are imposed at the object list level. If a change is required on a single page, only that page, not the entire form, needs to be re-RIPed and then substituted back into the imposition. This gives the functionality of ROOM and NORM without tying the system up processing imposition-size files, which can often be hundreds of megabytes in size.

Task Integration in RIPs
One of the most important advances in workflow technology has come through the inclusion and automation of repetitive production tasks within the RIP itself. This allows needed alterations to be made to jobs without the need for operator intervention and moves processing-intensive tasks away from individual workstations, resulting in saved time and money.

Most new RIPs today are shipped with the capability for in-RIP separation. Instead of preseparating images and files into CMYK format, these RIPs are able to accept RGB data and convert to CMYK on the fly. This lends support to the trend to move toward RGB workflows, beneficial when images must be used for multiple printing processes or be repurposed for multimedia or Internet applications.

One of the newest features to be added to RIPs is the ability to trap files within the RIP. Trapping color breaks is a time-intensive process in which colors that touch each other, called abutting colors, are slightly expanded so that the two colors barely overprint each other. This avoids problems that can occur from misregistration on press. Automated trapping solutions are seeing more use as the complexity of digitally created designs exceeds the ability to manually trap files.

Some RIP manufacturers for digital presses allow the RIP to be connected directly to the Internet or a network. If on-line pages need to be printed, the operator simply sends the appropriate address to the RIP, which then seeks out the page on the Internet or internal network, downloads it, RIPs it, and prints it. This feature has many implications for future document-management solutions, where a company may need to keep only a single copy of its internal documentation on a network server, which can be available to whoever needs access.

The expansion of responsibilities within the RIP has led some companies to adopt a different approach toward this technology. RIPs that contain multiple internal features are sometimes referred to as reconfigurable image processors because they are capable of performing far more than mere rasterization of a page. The vision of these companies is to have a fully configurable system that can be changed as different jobs are destined for different imaging devices or print processes.

Task integration in RIPs should not be confused with workflow servers, which combine multiple programs—usually including a RIP—on a single server. For example, there is a difference between a RIP that traps files and a workflow server that includes trapping software. In-RIP options are relatively new innovations and suffer from a lack of experience on the part of printers. Nonetheless, these options highlight the trend toward consolidation of multiple production tasks within a single device.

Chapter 13

Marking Engines

Unless work is being created for Internet or multimedia publishing, the ultimate intent of any graphic arts work is to print the piece. Up until a few years ago this meant exclusively using one of the four major processes: lithography, gravure, flexography, or screen printing. With advances in technology, we now have many options for printing that were previously unavailable. Though many pieces are still printed using traditional methods, options like digital presses, inkjets, and advances in platesetting technology provide a variety of choices for final output.

Regardless of method, at some point in the process, ink must be applied to paper or film must be exposed. At the heart of these devices is a marking engine. Quite simply, a marking engine is any device intended to create images on some media. Any marking engine will fall generically into one of several categories: toner-based devices, inkjet devices, imagesetters, or platesetters. Though there is a wide variety of options available in devices within each category, they all share some fundamental similarities that allow us to place each in perspective.

Toner-Based Devices
From fax machines to laser printers to four-color digital presses, toner-based marking engines are fast becoming one of the most common ways to get material printed. Toner devices are an offshoot of copiers, using many of the same fundamental concepts to get images and text onto paper. The basic technology at work is electrophotography—using electricity and light to create latent

images on a photoconductive material, transferring the image onto paper, and then fusing or fixing the image permanently onto the paper.

The center of a toner-based machine is a photoconductor. A photoconductor is a material that conducts electricity in the presence of light. By charging a photoconductor in darkness and then applying light only in selected areas, a latent image can be created electrically on a photoconductor. In a copier, the light is reflected off an original and through a set of lenses onto the photoconductor. In a laser printer or digital press, a laser, modulated from digital data, is used to "etch" away the electrostatic charge from the photoconductor.

Once the latent image has been created, oppositely charged toner is applied to the photoconductor. Toner is essentially a plastic material in particles that are approximately 10 microns (a micron is a millionth of a meter) in size. Because opposite electrical charges attract each other, toner is drawn wherever a charge exists on the photoconductor.

After the toner has been applied to the photoconductor, a piece of paper is allowed to come into contact with it. By again using the properties of electrostatics to oppositely charge the paper, the toner is transferred from the photoconductor to the paper. Once the transfer is complete, the paper is sent through a set of very hot rollers, which fixes the image permanently to the paper, called fusing. The photoconductor is then cleaned of any residual toner particles, and the process begins again.

Most laser printers and digital presses use a cylindrical photoconductor, called a drum. This geometry allows the drum to rotate while the charging and toner units remain fixed—an efficient process where many prints at high speeds are a requirement.

Newer high-speed digital presses use a long belt instead of a drum for a photoconductor. Four in-line toner-application modules are then placed along the belt. As paper is moved with the belt, toner is transferred to the sheet, increasing the printing speed by four times.

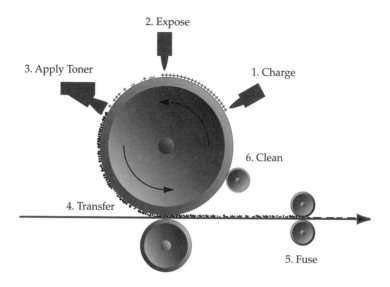

Laser printers use a photoconductive drum, which is cleaned after each impression.

Some processes use a liquid toner—toner particles dispersed in kerosene or a kerosene derivative. The advantage to liquid toner systems is in resolution. Liquid toner particles are only 2 or 3 microns in size as opposed to the 10-micron size of dry toner particles. Though at first glance the difference in size between 10 and 2 microns may seem trivial, the resolution of dry toner systems is limited due to their size, and liquid toner systems have noticeably higher resolutions.

Inkjet Printers
Inkjets have become increasingly popular as personal printers. They are relatively simple in design, and so the lowest-end models can be purchased for sometimes as little as $100 for a color printer. In contrast to inexpensive inkjet printers, some of the highest quality proofing devices available are inkjet printers. Inkjets come in several varieties. The difference in cost and quality comes from the type of ink-feeding system.

Whereas laser printers are generally very complex, inkjets are really very simple. A water-based dye is held in a reservoir. As a sheet of paper is transported through the device, the head moves back and forth across the surface of the paper, spitting out droplets of ink on the paper. Because the dyes used are water based, or aqueous, once the water evaporates from the paper, the dye colorants are left behind. There is no need for any fixing or fusing system in inkjet printers.

The simplest form of inkjet is a thermal inkjet. In these systems there is a heating element in the bottom of the ink reservoir. To distribute ink onto the paper, the heating element is charged. As the reservoir heats, a vapor bubble is formed and expands within the reservoir. This expansion forces a droplet of ink onto the paper.

The second type of inkjet is a piezoelectric or drop-on-demand system. The ink reservoir is connected to a series of tiny electronics that form a matrix through which ink can pass. By varying the charge, ink droplets are forced out of the reservoir and onto the paper.

The most expensive and high-quality inkjets use a continuous-feed inking system. In these systems the inks are electrically charged and allowed to constantly flow from the reservoir. Electrical conductors are placed at the exit point of the ink reservoir. By adjusting the charge of these conductors, the inks are either allowed to travel to the paper or deflected into a waste-storage collector. Continuous-feed systems are expensive devices to purchase because of the electronics involved and are also expensive in consumables.

Inkjet inks are all expensive, and the continuous-feed systems often send as much ink into the waste collector as they do onto the paper. Despite this, they can produce extraordinarily high-quality prints.

Many of the common problems associated with inkjets come from the fact that they use aqueous inks. If too much ink is placed onto the paper, it tends to curl or distort from water absorption, called cockle. Specialty coated papers can limit paper cockle—but at a much higher cost than normal bond paper. In some cases, plastic-based rather than cellulose-based substrates are used.

Another method commonly used to limit this problem is converting colors in the printing software to use the minimum possible ink required. This is achieved by converting images back to RGB, then reseparating them into CMYK using 100% gray component replacement.

Though this conversion is not problematic for low-end devices that do not attempt critical color reproduction, high-end color suffers if images are altered as they are printed. Overall, inkjet printers tend to be less expensive than laser printers in the initial purchase but more expensive for consumables. The popularity of inkjets comes primarily from the fact that they are easily affordable color printers for home use.

Imagesetters
Imagesetters are used to expose film for printing from a digital file. The first imagesetters developed from laser typesetting machines. These devices allowed the user to key in text, which was then exposed to film using a laser. As desktop publishing developed, it was relatively simple to modify typesetting imagers to receive page data and thus image an entire page rather than merely galleys of type to be manually stripped in to the flats.

The first imagesetters were capstan devices. In a capstan imagesetter, film is advanced at a specific speed by a set of rollers. The laser remains stationary and scans across the width of the film as it moves past. Capstan imagesetters are still made and used in the industry but are not as common as newer types of imagesetters. Because the film moves past the laser, it can be difficult to achieve perfect registration when imaging multicolor work.

In an effort to improve the registration issues involved with capstan devices, external drum imagesetters were developed that used a different method for transporting the film through the machine. Instead of constantly moving the film, film was advanced onto a cylindrical drum and held there by a vacuum system. The drum then rotated, moving the film across a laser. The mounting mechanism that placed the film onto the drum allowed images to be precisely registered from color to color.

Even with external drum imagesetters, there were some problems with registration. As the drum rotated, it had the potential to suffer from vibrations that could cause slight misalignment of register. The solution to this problem was to mount the film inside a stationary drum and then move the laser across the surface of the film.

These engines, known as internal drum imagesetters, provide the highest level of registration in imagesetters. The laser is mounted on a screw mechanism that moves through the center of the drum.

A rotating mirror controls the laser around the circumference of the drum, while at the same time the laser is slowly advanced across the width of the drum.

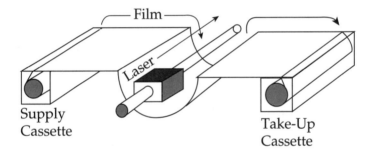

An internal drum imagesetter.

At the same time that different film transport methods were being developed for imagesetters, the size of imagesetters was also being increased. The first capstan devices could image a single 8.5x11-inch page at a time. This still required each page to be manually stripped in, or positioned, in place to create the final printing form. It was quickly realized that increasing the size of imagesetters would save a tremendous amount of labor time by reducing the amount of manual assembly that had to be done. Imagesetters were released that could image a two-page spread at one time, reducing the manual assembly time by nearly half.

Once internal drum engines were released, it was possible to build imagesetters that could expose full four- or eight-page flats at one time. This met the needs of companies using most presses, which can handle sheets either 30 or 40 inches in width. These imagesetters were nicknamed "imposetters" because they were capable of imaging a full imposition in a single exposure.

Many times, imagesetter size is referred to by the number of 8.5x11-inch pages it is possible to image at one time. Imposetters capable of running 30-inch film are termed four-up imagesetters because they can image four 8.5x11 pages with bleeds and marks at one exposure. Forty-inch imposetters are commonly referred to as eight-up devices. Imposetters are available in sizes exceeding 60 inches in width.

Platesetters

The motivation behind increasing the size of imagesetters is to reduce the amount of manual assembly that must be performed on film before it is ready for platemaking. The obvious extension of this idea is to create devices that are capable of imaging the plates directly. This technology is now well on its way to being implemented as computer-to-plate systems. Though platesetters are similar to imagesetters in their basic technologies, there are some difficulties that exist in imaging comparably stiff aluminum plates that were not critical in imaging film.

The first type of platesetter was a flatbed device. The plate remained on a flat surface while the laser was directed by a set of mirrors and lenses across the surface. The major limitation to flatbed platesetters is in maintaining a consistent-size dot on the plate. As the laser images areas farther away from the center of the plate, the laser spot becomes dimensionally distorted. Imagine holding a flashlight at waist level and shining it straight down at the ground. The light will be circular and consistent. As you angle the flashlight farther away from center, the light becomes more elliptical than circular. In a laser exposure system, this would result in inconsistent dots on the plate near its edges. Though lens systems were used to correct for this, they could not entirely remove the inconsistencies. Flatbed platesetters therefore have size limitations.

Dots become distorted as the angle changes from light source to media.

A second platesetter technology similar to the development of imagesetters was to mount the plate using an internal drum system. Though this is the most effective technology for imaging film, metallic plates have a reflective property that is not encountered when imaging film. Not all the laser light is absorbed by the plate material. The resulting scattering of light causes unwanted exposure in random areas on the plate.

Again echoing the development of imagesetters, external drum platesetters were developed. External drum engines have proven to be very effective as platesetters. The plates can be easily fed from a cassette, mounted on the drum and, after exposure, moved to a processor. The biggest advantage to external drum devices is that because the drum is rotated across the laser, the laser can be placed very close to the surface of the drum.

The biggest cost in platesetters is the laser. The farther away from the drum the laser is placed, the more power is required from the laser, and the higher the cost of the laser. In external drum platesetters the laser is so close to the drum that low-cost lasers can be used for exposure. The result is a much lower-priced machine.

Polyester and Paper Plates
Though the vast majority of plates used in lithography are made from anodized aluminum, there are many cases where it is appropriate to use a polyester- or cellulose-based plate material. In these cases, the distinction between imagesetters and platesetters becomes blurred. Many imagesetters are capable of imaging polyester plates and cellulose plates as well as resin-coated paper, requiring only that the new material be loaded into a cassette or other feed mechanism and that the device be recalibrated for sensitivity differences in the materials.

One of the more interesting developments in platesetting devices is the use of toner to generate a plate. The base requirement of a lithographic image carrier is that there be a chemical differentiation between the image areas and the nonimage areas where image areas are oleophilic, or oil-attracting, and nonimage areas are hydrophilic, or water-attracting. Because toner particles have oleophilic properties, if toner is printed onto a hydrophilic material the resulting print can be used effectively as a plate.

Many quick printers use toner-based platesetters that are essentially laser printers that have been modified to accept a specialized plate material. This provides an inexpensive way to generate plates for work where tight registration or high screen rulings is not a requirement.

Thermal Imaging Systems
One of the newest advances in platesetting technology is the use of thermal energy rather than visible light energy for exposure.

Thermal systems have the advantage of providing a harder dot structure on the plate, as well as avoiding possible over- or under-exposure of materials. The differences in visible-light and thermal systems come mostly from the sensitivity of the materials.

Materials that expose to visible light allow additivity to exposure. In other words, as more energy is applied to traditional materials, exposure increases. Exposure in these systems is a function both of intensity and time.

A simple way to understand this is by using another flashlight analogy. Imagine that you have two flashlights: one that emits 1,000 "units" of energy in 1 second, another that emits 100 "units" of energy in one second. Shining the "1,000-unit" flashlight on a piece of film or plate material for one second produces the exact same exposure as shining the "100-unit" flashlight on a piece of film or plate material for 10 seconds.

Both cases result in 1,000 energy units reaching the film. What is critical to the understanding of visible-light imaging is that this exposure does not have to be concurrent. We could shine the 100-unit flashlight on the film for one second each day, and in ten days we will have reached the desired exposure on the film.

Though a laser provides the most consistent light source available, even laser light is not 100% consistent across the entire area of the spot on the plate. This means that in visible-light systems there will always be a soft area around each dot, called the dot fringe, where slight exposure has taken place. This causes a reduction in print quality by unavoidably increasing the size of each dot. Visible-light systems always have this problem with dot fringe (see the illustration on the second page following).

Materials that expose to thermal energy, however, are not additive. These materials have a built-in trigger point that must be reached before they will react to exposure. Further, once that trigger point has been reached, the materials expose completely, avoiding any chance of overexposure.

Imagine that we again have two flashlights, except this time we have one flashlight that emits energy at 1,000 degrees and one flashlight that emits energy at 100 degrees. We are trying to expose a thermal material with a trigger point of 900 degrees. Shining the 1,000-degree flashlight on the material for even a moment will cause the material to expose completely. But if we try to use the 100-degree flashlight this time, the material will never expose. No matter how long we subject the material to the 100-degree energy, we will never reach the trigger point of the material. Thermal imaging systems provide a dot structure that is much harder—a dot that has no fringe.

There is still some argument in the industry as to whether or not thermal systems actually produce better presswork. Though there is no doubt that they produce harder dots on the plate, this does not automatically translate into an immediate improvement in printing conditions.

A valid point is that a printing system operating in an environment with a good set of process controls can produce good presswork, regardless of whether thermal or visible light lasers are used to expose the plate. It is more important that dot gain and other tone-reproduction characteristics are accounted for. Ignoring these attributes will cause problems on the press regardless of the imaging technology used to create the plate.

Thermal plates also require a baking process if they are to be used for extremely long runs. After imaging and processing, the plate is placed into a heated chamber. This "sets" the polymers on the aluminum, letting the plates last for run lengths up to 100,000 impressions. Whether this is an issue or not depends entirely upon the type of work produced within the company.

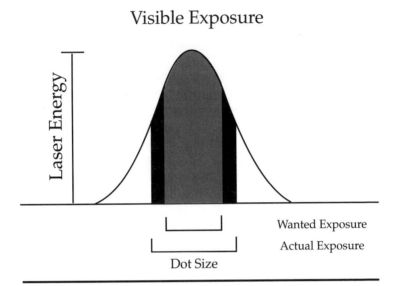

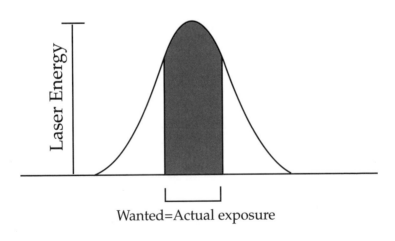

Thermal systems result in less dot fringe from unwanted exposure.

Despite the proven differences in dot structure between thermal and visible-light systems, there is still much lively debate in the industry as to whether this creates an appreciable difference in actual print quality. Proponents of visible-light systems point out that with proper calibration, visible-light systems are capable of producing equal print quality to thermal systems; that there is inherent dot fringe in printing anyway due to dot gain from ink absorption to the paper; and that thermal plates often require an additional baking step in order to increase the usable life of the plate.

Though many printers have chosen thermal computer-to-plate systems, many visible-light systems are still sold and used in the industry.

Direct Imaging and Digital Presses
Direct imaging and digital presses are a continuation of the trend in the industry toward moving the imaging process closer and closer to the press. In these devices the image carrier is exposed directly on the press, removing any need for external imagesetting or platesetting. Though both devices share this attribute, there are also important distinctions between these two types of devices.

A direct imaging press uses a static image carrier that is exposed directly on the press. These presses use traditional lithographic inks. In fact, the first digital imaging press was a standard press that had its dampening systems replaced with roller-fed plate and exposure units. Direct imaging presses provide quality levels that approach standard lithography and are excellent for applications where high-quality, short-run work is required.

A digital press uses an image carrier, which is exposed separately for each impression. Most digital presses are dry toner–based devices that have been modified with multiple drums or toner-application systems that allow them to reach acceptable speeds. Though digital presses have quality limitations in comparison to standard lithography, this is purely a relative comparison.

Digital presses are capable of producing excellent levels of work. In addition, the advantage of a dynamic image carrier for each impression allows opportunities that are impossible with any other process. Digital presses are directly responsible for the development of variable-data printing, a process whereby printed pieces are completely personalized by creating a relationship between a set of objects and a database. As a variable-data job is printed, each piece changes depending on the fields in the database that have been linked to printable objects. More and more, digital presses are being recognized as a potential future for the printing industry.

Chapter 14

Digital Beyond Prepress

When we consider digital technology in the graphic arts, most often we look at it from the aspect of prepress production. And though most of the changes involving digital data have been in this area, there is no reason to believe that the digital trend will end there. The digital revolution affects all aspects of the industry, from the design process through finishing. A basic conceptual shift has occurred that has changed the way we look at a document, its organization, and its life cycle. Approaches taken from database management have introduced a new term to the industry: document management.

Digital data is being used to track jobs, communicate with customers, automate processes, and to essentially reinvent publishing as new mediums for communications become widespread. Though the digital revolution has made radical changes to the graphic arts community in the last fifteen years, it has really only just begun.

Redefining the Document

The traditional document was very simple: text and graphics on a printed page, produced in mass quantities to save costs, stored for long periods of time, and distributed to final destinations as needed. It was common for companies to throw away thousands of printed pieces that had been inventoried until the document became obsolete. As new documents were needed, they went through a well-defined creative and production process. Each document stood on its own as a finite piece of work.

In the digital environment, a document is more correctly considered to be a process rather than a piece. A document can be a printed piece, or it can maintain its life cycle entirely within the digital domain. It can be made up not only of text and graphics but can also include movies, animations, sound clips, forms, scripts, databases, hypertext links, and it can even include other documents. As more channels are available to send and receive information, the document becomes more complex, frequently needing to be repurposed from one medium—print, for example—to another medium, like the Internet.

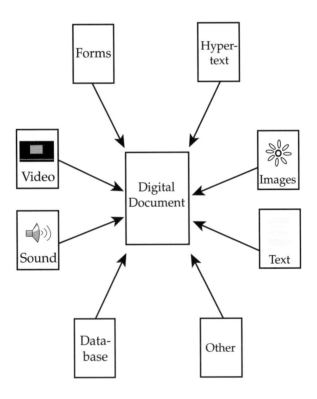

A modern document can contain many components.

The creative process has become much more integrated. Wide-area networks allow people from different parts of the world to work together toward the creation of a single document. The process may draw on the talents of a wide variety of different people, from traditional print providers to database and information technology managers. It is more common that a new document will not begin from scratch but will encompass and add to the information included in previous documents.

The logistics involved in document distribution have changed from digital influences. The traditional print, store, and distribute paradigm makes no sense in the modern world, and many companies are refusing to pay the costs of warehousing and distributing paper documents. Instead of print-and-distribute, companies are beginning the process of distribute-and-print. Digital presses are making it possible for businesses to electronically send their documents to the final location, print only as many as are needed at that time, and then locally distribute the final pieces.

From a workflow perspective, the changing definition of the document has far more implications than simply affecting prepress production. To be effective, workflow must be considered as an end-to-end process that allows the flexibility of the modern document process to take place while at the same time preventing chaos by providing structured command and control procedures that create logical, seamless progression through each necessary step.

Document Management

Traditional document creation was a linear process with clearly defined roles and steps. People worked together as a concise group, passing the document to the next stage of the process only after the preceding stage was completed. Today's creative environment is far more complex, both in process and content. Creation does not need to be linear; multiple tasks can be performed in parallel and brought together at the end of the process.

In a networked environment, many people in different locations may be working in concert on a document that resides on a single server. Document-management systems provide a method for verifying what has been done to a document and what needs to be done to a document, and provide version control over the document. This can be as simple as a check-out/check-in procedure to ensure that only one person at a time has control of the document, or it can be a complex system that uses preprogrammed logic to route the document through the process. Regardless of system, the complexities of maintaining a central server require some control structure, or work inevitably will be lost as people isolated from each other are unable to determine what stage of the process the document is currently in.

Document-management systems, like any workflow-related system, must be tailored to the environments within which they will function. If only printed pieces are to be created, then the system might have to track only image, illustration, text, and layout files. In a multimedia environment, the system will have to also keep track of audio, video, and hypertext files.

Job Tickets and Tracking

A workflow system needs to be capable of moving a job through a logical series of tasks. Job-ticket and tracking systems allow this logic to be established as part of the input procedures for the work. The electronic job-ticket file becomes the logic header for the job through the system. Each person doing each task in the workflow, or the workflow manager, can check the job ticket to determine what has been done and the next task that needs to be done.

Because different jobs require different procedures, job tickets provide a way to input logic to the workflow. For instance, a single-color job will require preflighting, imposition, and imaging. A complex multicolor job may require preflighting, scanning, random proofs generated, and a hold placed on the job until color approval is submitted, then imposition, imaging, and perhaps a second set of positional proofs with the job again held until approval is received. Inputting this information at the start of the process, perhaps in the estimating stage, allows automatic scheduling to take place as well.

Production scheduling is a difficult exercise in logistics that has to follow the rule that all jobs are important, but sometimes some jobs are more important than others. Scheduling must take into account deadlines as well as resources, with the ultimate goal of keeping everyone busy and keeping all the machines occupied. Tying a scheduling system into a job-tracking system can provide automation to the resource-management requirements of a production scheduling system.

Customers also need to be kept informed of the progress of their job through the production system. A tracking system that reports data as tasks are completed, as well as updating the production schedule, can be tied into a Web server that has password security features for customer access. This provides customers with an easily accessible report of their jobs' status.

Materials and Labor Tracking
Another area in which digital data can be beneficial is in tracking inventory, materials, and labor for each job. Not only must materials be tracked for each job, but the inventory for the entire plant must also be regulated. Accurate costing must be kept so that estimated versus actual analysis, comparing the actual cost of a job to the estimated cost, can measure profitability. These systems are normally segmented from the production workflow systems, but applying data from the job-ticket specifications can create a system where the scheduling and ordering of materials such as paper and ink can be tied in to the production schedule of the job.

Materials systems should also take into account the labor requirements for each job. As all aspects of job production become integrated into a single connected system, more logic structures can be written that will route each job not only through the production center of a plant but also through the planning and financial centers of the plant. The goal is to provide a single unified system that can address all the requirements of the job with a single logic input to a digital job ticket.

The movement of altering workflow to include aspects of job creation outside of the production center is similar to the adjustments needed in document management. Just as creative systems must account for a greater variety of file and document types, production workflow systems must be able to integrate tasks like estimating and material ordering if they are to be expected to accurately control job scheduling.

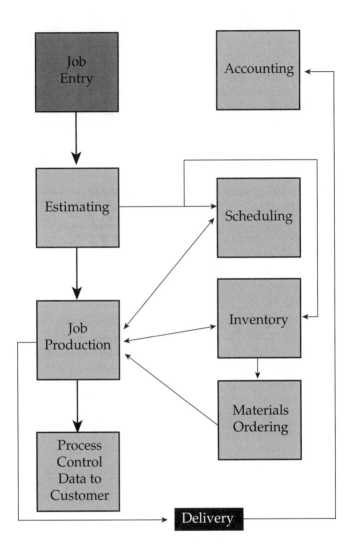

Integrated workflows use digital information across the entire process.

Press and Post-Press Control

Once an imposed job is processed by the RIP, all information needed for the press and finishing areas is contained within the imposed digital file. Exact sheet size, position of the work, number and type of colors, and ink coverage can all be interpolated out of the single imposed file. If finishing specifications like binding style are added through the use of a job ticket, it is possible to have the RIP create the data needed for setup by the press and finishing areas.

A part of the press make-ready process is to preset the ink zones on the press to shorten the time needed to bring the job up to color. Because most new presses have digital control units, the RIP can be used to create a data file that accurately represents ink coverage for each unit.

Uploading that data file to the press can automate much of the make-ready process and reduce the time needed to ready the press for printing. This can also be achieved by a separate device used to scan each plate and create an ink-zone preset file. Though this is not as efficient as having the RIP generate the data, it exceeds attempting to visually assess ink coverage and adjust the ink zones.

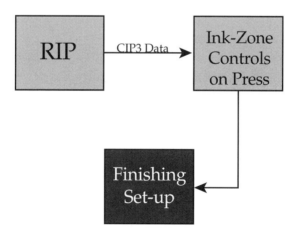

CIP3 data is designed to control press and post-press operations.

By knowing the press sheet size and the position of the work on the sheet, files can be created that will set up finishing equipment to properly process the printed press sheet. The Consortium for the Integration of Prepress, Press, and Postpress, known as CIP3 (pronounced "sip-three"), is a body whose members include most of the major graphic arts equipment manufacturers. CIP3 has established a standard for files that can be used to transmit press and finishing specifications to the appropriate pieces of equipment.

There are enormous time savings to taking advantage of digital controls by using preset files. If the RIP is connected by network to the press and finishing areas, an operator can simply open the appropriate job-control file on the equipment and begin running the job. Once color has been approved on a press, the current ink zone settings can be resaved as another data file and then archived with the job. This allows reprints of the same job at a later date with a high level of color matching to the previous run.

Digital data can also be supplied to customers to verify that their jobs were run within specified tolerances. Technology-savvy print buyers are actually requesting that this data—instead of hand-selected samples—be sent to them so they can statistically verify the quality of their jobs.

Chapter 15

Tasks in a Digital Production Workflow

Moving a shop to a totally digital workflow forces an implicit change in the conception of how work gets done. Often, as companies make the shift to digital, tasks in this new system are defined within the boundaries of traditional roles, but this approach can cause more problems than it solves. The issue is not just that certain jobs are completely eliminated; the technology requires us to consider that what used to be discrete jobs in the workflow need to be organized into new categories of responsibility. In order to be efficient, tasks need to be organized by what needs to get done rather than by who needs to do it.

This also implies that the traditional roles played by the operators in the workflow must be changed. Very few printers, if any, still have a functioning typesetting department—typesetting has been absorbed into the creative realm. An output technician with years of experience optimizing files may be better suited to create digital impositions in the new workflow than a former stripper. That same stripper may find a home in production planning.

Defining new roles for employees based on past workflows places limits on the system that can be counterproductive to achieving optimal efficiency. At the same time, companies must proactively seek ways to place employees to take the best advantage of their knowledge.

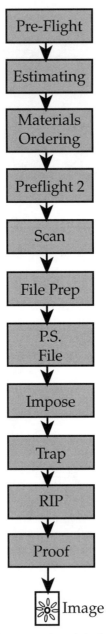

There are multiple tasks a job must go through in the production process.

The basic unit of a workflow is a task. A task needs to be a finite action; it must have a measurable beginning and end. This may seem excessively basic, but as tasks become connected and decisions must be made as to which set of tasks must be followed to complete a project, the proper categorization of each individual task must be in place to implement a structured process logic.

The success of the overall system will depend primarily on whether each component has been well ordered. A breakdown in logic at the component level will affect the entirety of the system.

Though component tasks must be broken down into basic units of work, the organization must not be overly restrictive. Preflighting and archiving, for example, need to be separate tasks within the workflow. But breaking preflight up into steps such as load the fonts, open the file, and generate a report only adds unnecessary complexity to the logical workflow decisions that must be made. A set of standard operating procedures should exist for each task, but this should be kept separate from the issue of job control between tasks.

The potential for automation also needs to be kept in mind as basic tasks are organized. Printing is a job-based manufacturing industry, which means that some decisions about jobs will always inherently require human intervention. Other repetitive tasks in the workflow can often be automated. This frees up the most valuable assets in the company—the employees—to focus their time in making better decisions where they need to be made.

Creation
A great deal of the success of any digital job depends on the care with which it is created. Ask anyone with experience in outputting files if you doubt that jobs can be created digitally that are completely unprintable. Even though the bulk of this task lies outside the walls of the printing plant, the printer can, and should, provide input to the creative process. A digital workflow begins at the creative level. Mistakes made here will delay the entrance of the job into the production line.

A well-trained sales and customer service representative staff, along with accessible technology experts within the company, should go out of their way to provide tactful advice to a designer. Likewise, designers should have no reticence in communicating with their printers to get needed information about their specific printing characteristics. This doesn't just help the workflow; it can promote a partnership that ties the creator to the printer.

Preflight

The term "preflight," borrowed from aviation, is a thorough check of a digital file before it enters the production workflow. Have all fonts been sent? Are supplied images and artwork there and in the correct formats? Have the correct colors been specified in the file? If a file does not match the written specifications, the discrepancy needs to be resolved before proceeding.

Software packages exist that can contribute a level of automation to this process, provided that the person reading the generated reports has sufficient expertise in the requirements of the prepress department.

The importance of the preflight process cannot be overstated. If job production is to be efficient, incoming materials must meet a specified level of conformancy. Many creative firms are establishing preflight checks as the final stage in their process before sending a file to a printer. This helps to prevent jobs from incurring costly charges for author alterations due to simple oversight errors.

Image Capture

Traditionally, image capture has meant the digitization of photographs and line art, but a digital workflow places entirely new emphasis in this area. Any art not submitted on disk must be digitized if it is ever to see the press. This may mean the purchase of new equipment—a copy-dot scanner is required to convert existing film into files that can be imaged with a computer-to-plate system.

Much of the burden of transition between workflows will fall in this area as legacy work—work that has been stored in an analog format—is moved into the digital domain. Image capture is an optional step in the workflow. Workflow logic needs to accommodate the potential for skipping this step. Image capture in the workflow may also need to be connected to the archiving/retrieval task set if images from a previous job need to be included in an incoming job. Image capture should also link directly into an internal proofing/correction cycle so that color can be verified before the job progresses to the next stage of the workflow.

Page Preparation
This represents the stage at which all files are brought together into a composite page and converted into PostScript or some other intermediary file format for further processing. Color breaks, type flow, page geometry, and image positioning are all manually evaluated and adjusted as needed to assure that they meet specifications. Page assembly can be a major source of bottlenecks in the production workflow, as it is often difficult to assess the exact amount of time needed to complete this stage.

This stage can also be considered an advanced level of preflight. The original preflight verifies that all basic components of the job are supplied. The page-assembly stage requires that a knowledgeable technician manually check that the file meets the expectations for the intended printing conditions. This is an essential operation.

Though it could be argued that page preparation and the output of files as PostScript or intermediaries are two separate operations, for the sake of efficiency it makes sense to perform both of these tasks at the same stage. Once page preparation is completed, the file is ready to progress to the next stage. Separating these operations only increases handoffs, potential communications errors, and increased burden on the network, workstations, and the trained staff needed to perform this operation.

File Repair
It is possible that the page-preparation process will indicate that there are problems that require major repairs to a file. If this is the case, file repair should be treated as a separate step in the workflow. Though the page-preparation stage requires a more advanced level of knowledge than the original preflight, most incoming files follow a relatively routine structure that can be taught even to a novice desktop operator.

File repair, however, is a task that often requires the resources of the most highly trained operators available, people who completely understand the complexities and nuances of working with digital artwork. Setting file repair apart from other processes also helps in financial accounting of charges that may be incurred at this stage.

Notice that the preflight/page preparation/file repair organization also creates a hierarchy that gradually leads a job into more advanced levels of processing only if it is required. This helps to assure that the most valuable people in the operation are not wasting their time checking for things like missing fonts. Splitting technical resources can provide a background for training structure, as well as preventing the problem of housing all technical knowledge in a plant within only a few people.

Image Swapping

The size of digital images mandates some strategy for controlling the flow of these files across the network. It is likely that any plant faced with this situation needs to integrate some form of OPI for swapping low-resolution FPO images with server-stored high-resolution images. Image swapping should be a concise step in the workflow with a structured series of procedures outlining the process.

OPI is always a two-part strategy. At some point, high-resolution images need to be first placed onto an image server. This may or may not generate low-resolution proxy files, depending on whether the job is still in the creative stage or if it has already passed into production.

The second part of an OPI strategy involves the actual swap of high-res for low-res files. This will always be automated at the server level, though it may require making some adjustments at the page-preparation stage. Despite the automation of this stage, workflow must account for OPI as a two-part process.

Imposition

Imposition is the organization of individual pages into correct positioning for the press form or signature. Once relegated entirely to strippers manually taping film to sheets of mylar, imposition layouts themselves do not change in the digital workflow, though the method of accomplishing them does. Imposition software can be stand-alone on a workstation, or it can be integrated into some proprietary solution.

There are multiple strategies available for imposition. The simplest involves the use of stand-alone software running on a workstation. If this is the case, it may make sense to combine imposition directly with the page-preparation stage of the workflow. Again, this limits handoffs, communications errors, and network burden. If a job is already on a workstation, it should be fully processed there, if possible.

Most high-end proprietary systems include a method for imposing forms from pre-RIPed intermediate files. This allows late changes to individual pages to be made without having to open, verify, and re-RIP entire forms for simple changes. Known as late-binding systems, this can be a powerful addition to this stage of the workflow and should be implemented if your system supports it.

Trapping
Wherever two different colors touch on a form, one must be enlarged so that a small overlap occurs. This corrects for slight registration problems on the press and prevents the paper from showing through gaps between colors. Trapping is dynamic within the workflow. It can be done at the creation stage, within page assembly, or performed on entire impositions with special software dedicated solely to this purpose.

The complexity with which digital art can be created has changed the focus on trapping. Though all page-layout programs support some level of trapping, none is fully effective. A complex digital workflow, especially in a computer-to-plate environment where traditional film trapping will be impossible, mandates the use of specialized software for this task. This assures that traps will be consistent for all page elements.

There is a limit to the amount of automation that can be expected from trapping software. Though automated workflows can be set up for jobs falling within broad categories, all four-color process work—for example, complex jobs using specialized colors—will need a skilled operator who fully understands the requirements of the press and the interactions of inks to create an effective trap.

Proofing
Digital proofing is one of the most complex areas within a work-flow. Proofing generally falls into three categories: preliminary, contract color, and positional proofs. Traditionally, proofs were created from the same film that would be used to expose the plates.

The use of a static medium provided some guarantees that the proof was an accurate simulation of what would come off the press. Proofing solutions in the digital workflow will be determined by what the client is willing to accept. It requires some faith that the interpretation of the file by the proofer will match the interpretation of the file by the platesetter or press.

One of the controversies surrounding digital proofing is over dot-based versus continuous-tone proofs. Adequate solutions exist for both, though dot-based digital proofing is consistently more expensive than continuous-tone. Remote proofing and soft proofing are other contentious areas that allow proofs to be generated within the creative stage, but they can require a good deal of client training to be effective.

Many of the workflow complexities in proofing come from assigning various types of proofs to a particular stage of the workflow. For example, preliminary proofs are required at the image-capture stage. These proofs could also be used as contract color proofs, or contract proofs could be generated later after the imposition stage. Organizing a proofing strategy is consistently one of the more difficult aspects of digital workflows.

Proofing stages must also always direct the job into at least two other potential tasks. The job must first be held until the proof is approved. That hold-for-approval process needs to be approached as a concise step in the workflow that may occur a number of times in the job cycle. Proofing must also have the potential to lead into a correction cycle, which will itself lead back to the proofing and hold-for-approval stages.

Hold for Approval

It is essential that any action that needs to be performed on a job be accounted for in the logic structure of a workflow system. Hold for approval, though it does not designate a production action on a job, must be represented within the workflow. Itemizing tasks such as holding a job represents the conceptual change that must occur in the switch to a digital workflow.

Holding a job can occur at multiple points in the workflow, generally whenever a proof is sent out or a change in job specifications occurs. Creating a separate category for this stage also provides an opportunity to assess latency, time a job spends in a plant without work being done on it, by measuring the time a job spends on hold. In turn, understanding latency is key to shortening the cycle time of all jobs.

Raster Image Processing

The organization of the RIPing stage of the job will depend entirely upon the workflow system used in the plant. This is because proprietary systems split the RIPing process to generate intermediary files. In a traditional PostScript workflow, the RIPing stage will almost always occur directly between the output and imaging stages.

The RIP stage becomes more complex if proprietary workflow systems are used. Many of these systems make the RIPing process dynamic within the workflow to accommodate specific trapping, proofing, or imposition strategies. This logic block may have to be split into multiple stages depending on how you want your system to function.

Output/Imaging

The requirements for output vary depending on whether the device used is a proofer, platesetter, direct-to-press device, or digital press. There are, however, some similarities. Generally, output will be produced from the imposition stage rather than the page-assembly stage (though technically the generation of PostScript is a type of output, the term is used here to represent the imaging of a digital file onto some physical medium). The final output must also match the proof or create plates with which it will be possible to match the proof.

It is important to differentiate the exact type of output needed, and it may be necessary to create separate logic blocks depending on the requirements of the output device. Imaging film as spreads to be manually imposed should obviously be a separate step from imaging fully imposed film or plates. Likewise, outputting proofs will be separated from outputting plates.

Backup /Archiving

Backup and archiving are often confused within a workflow. Backup is the temporary storage of active files to protect against system failure. Archiving is the final storage of job files at the exit stage of the workflow. Both require that some choices be made. Will tape, CD-R, or DVD formats be used to store files? When will backup and archiving be performed? Will all files concerning the job be stored, or only the application files? How will archived files be referenced so that they can be easily found if needed a month or a year in the future?

Some companies use a database program like Filemaker or even an Excel spreadsheet to keep track of job locations. Digital files for printing are enormous, so even a small or medium-size shop needs to plan for a storage capacity measured in terabytes. Permanence is also a major issue—the loss of files from media failure can represent literally hundreds of thousands of dollars.

Backup and archiving should be represented as two distinct operations within the workflow. A third operation that needs to be accounted for is the retrieval of archived work. Though the same systems will be used for all three of these operations, because they represent different actions on a job that can occur at different stages, they must be logically distinguished from each other.

Information Systems

As the complexity of technology increases within a printing plant the task of information systems specialist becomes more and more important. Who will be relied on to maintain the network, servers, and workstations that act as the vascular system of the workflow? In a small or medium-size shop, this does not necessarily need to be a dedicated position, but it is important that the person given this responsibility is capable of the task.

There is a big difference between someone knowledgeable about using computers and software for printing and someone knowledgeable about the nuances of networking protocols and operating systems. Be certain that time and training is dedicated to maintaining the infrastructure of the workflow.

As your workflow system becomes more automated, it will become progressively more important to have someone on the staff who can handle scripting and networking responsibilities. Advanced workflow systems are much more a computer-science issue than a printing issue. Because the logic of software and workflow development is so similar, a dedicated information systems specialist may be able to provide a needed point of view toward the development of a fully automated workflow management system.

The addition of a specialized information systems employee also allows the company to begin approaching system and workflow development as a formalized process. Many of the problems that exist in production workflows are not from lack of equipment or knowledge; rather, it is simply that the workflow has been added to gradually as the company has grown, instead of being implemented as a single system. Approaching information systems problems with a formal methodology may alone increase efficiency enough to justify the cost.

Create Logic Blocks That Fit Your Structure
It is entirely likely that some of the actions defined above will not fit in all workflows, and just as likely that there will be actions taken on a job in a specific environment that are not listed above. There is no one single workflow solution for all companies. As you create the logic blocks from which your workflow will be built, be certain to take into account the structure, environment, and skill sets that make up your specific situation.

The most difficult issue in teaching workflow and process management is that in the graphic arts, all companies tend to share some attributes, but none is exactly the same. Your workflow needs to be approached as exactly that: *your* workflow. Every company has a different set of business demands, type of work, physical layout, and employee skill sets.

This is further aggravated by the fact that although many companies fall under the graphic arts umbrella, they perform varied activities within the process. An advertising agency, a prepress firm, and a commercial printer all work within the graphic arts, and they may all have the need to adjust their workflows. But their specific needs will be quite different from company to company. There simply is no single best answer to please everyone.

Begin the process by setting goals that meet the company's basic requirement: fulfilling the needs of its customers. Your customers' demands are what set the pace for all the work going through the shop. In fact, if these demands are being met easily and consistently, you may want to consider whether it is a good idea to change the workflow at all!

One of the easiest ways to get started is to follow jobs through their progress in the shop. Think about what actions are routinely performed on jobs, where they occur, and who is doing them. Workflow analysis is simply a logic problem, and like any logical analysis, once it is broken down into its most basic components the solutions begin to make themselves clear.

Chapter 16

Task Integration and Location

Once tasks within the production process have been isolated and broken into concise logic blocks, the next step is to look at reorganizing these logic blocks in a structure that provides maximum efficiency to the process. The reorganization process needs to take into account all the variables that exist within your specific environment: the type of business, the skill sets of employees, the type and capabilities of the equipment you own or wish to add, specific demands from customers, and the level of automation that will be required. In short, to effectively analyze and reorganize the workflow, every other aspect of the business environment will have to be addressed.

In workflow reengineering, this is the most important consideration. Remember that our intent is to adjust the business process to be efficient within the infrastructure of the shop. We are not just buying technology to patch a hole. That's how the problem developed. We are changing the process to prevent the "holes" from ever occurring.

One strategy that many companies find effective is to begin by surveying their customers. Ask them what they like and dislike about doing business with your company. This provides an in-depth starting point for establishing the goals around which the reengineering process will be developed. By getting this information from your customers, you ensure that your goals will provide real value enhancements to the business.

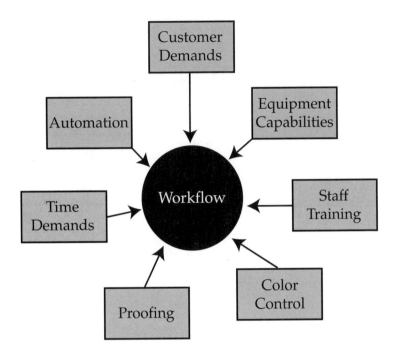

Workflow decisions must account for many variables in the process.

There are many different categories of printing, and each will have its own special workflow requirements. Commercial sheet-fed printing shops typically have a large quantity of jobs with relatively short run lengths, so special emphasis will have to be placed on preflight, proofing, and correction cycles. All these jobs must be co-ordinated, tracked, and accessed.

Newspapers and publications that operate with stringent deadlines may be more focused on cycle time. Workflow reorganization needs to be approached with specific goals in mind. "Making the workflow more efficient" is a noble goal, but it's too vague to be very useful. Make your workflow goals accomplishable so that you can measure your progress. "Creating a proofing and correction structure" is a manageable goal specific enough to guide the reorganization process.

Though some of the tasks will be relegated to automated equipment, many of the tasks within the workflow need to be performed, managed, or initiated by an employee. Do not forget the impact of individual employees on the workflow. Consider the special skills of each person in the production process before reorganizing a job out of existence. Finding out after that job has been eliminated that one of your employees provided a key quality-control check will be devastating to the reorganization effort.

If you plan to implement new equipment or reorganize around your existing equipment, this needs to be assessed before reorganizing your workflow. Post-RIP imposition strategies require equipment, special training, and a learning curve for implementation. The goal is to approach workflow reorganization as part of a single unified process. Look at all the equipment used in the process and evaluate the full capabilities of the equipment. You may be surprised to find when you do this that some equipment is being underutilized. Workflow changes require looking at possibilities, and the only way to do this is to know in advance what options are or will be available through the equipment.

Another important source of input for workflow restructuring is from your customers. Many times the goals for workflow restructuring include providing a greater level of customer service and responsiveness—in fact, this should always be the underlying goal of any change made to your business. Create a survey and distribute it to your best customers. Have your salespeople seek feedback about what your customers like and dislike about your process. Your customers will be pleased to see that you are proactively seeking ways to make their business process easier and will almost certainly provide a point of view that you have not fully considered.

Reorganization and Reengineering
Reengineering is one of the popular catch-phrases used in the printing industry about workflow. But workflow reengineering is not always appropriate, as it implies a complete change to the process. It is important to understand the difference between reorganizing and reengineering, as well as the three general motivations that cause a company to consider making changes in its workflow process.

Most workflow changes will be approached as restructuring rather than reengineering. Though the final goal may be to change all or most aspects of the production process, it should be done in finite steps according to a master plan. This is in opposition to a total reengineering plan, which will change at one time multiple aspects of the process.

The restructuring approach will almost always be the better approach because it takes into account that any change in the production workflow needs to be carefully considered, implemented, assessed for efficiency, and then any needed changes need to be made before moving on to the next stage. Making global haphazard changes to the workflow increases the risk that some overlooked aspect will cause more damage than improvement to the process.

There are three overall motivations for approaching workflow changes. The worst motivation for workflow change is a catastrophic breakdown of the process. In this situation, the process has been allowed to degrade to the point at which it simply can no longer efficiently support getting work through the system. It is hoped this will never be the case, as other key indicators should have outlined a problem in the process long before it reaches this state. Nonetheless, in the day-to-day stress of getting work done, many companies find it difficult to budget the time necessary to periodically evaluate their system, resulting in a catastrophic failure. This situation may require a complete reengineering if efficiency has already degraded to this point.

Workflow changes can be motivated by one or two single goals. A company may seek simply to improve its proofing strategies or change the way job progress through the plant is tracked. A goal-oriented approach to workflow restructuring seeks to change only certain aspects of the total process.

Proper analysis of the workflow in its entirety is still a requirement even in a goal-oriented approach. Any manufacturing process, including printing, is subject to multiple dependencies in the workflow. What happens in a single stage will have reverberating effects downstream and possibly upstream from that stage. Any change must be carefully considered in terms of its effects on connected processes.

By far the best case for workflow restructuring is to include it as a part of a plan for continual process improvement. Companies should be consistently measuring and analyzing their processes, always looking for areas of improvement. Including workflow restructuring as a part of the overall process-improvement plan means that all factors that affect the business will inherently be taken into account for the workflow plan. A company that is dedicated to following a process-improvement plan will rarely, if ever, fall into the catastrophic category.

If your company does not already have a process-improvement initiative in place, workflow analysis will often provide the structure and information needed to begin this process. As companies in the graphic arts struggle to remain competitive within the changing technology and business environment of today, many are finding that formalized process improvement is directly allowing them to reduce costs and find ways to differentiate themselves from their competitors. If your intent is to do the level of work needed to correctly evaluate and restructure your production workflow, it makes sense to take advantage of the background information you will generate by initiating a simultaneous process-improvement plan.

Organizing Participants in the Workflow
Workflow is not simply a jumble of different tasks. Each task will require a participant to perform, manage, or initiate the action. The participant may be a human being, or it may be a machine. As tasks are organized and considered, a large part of the process will include an analysis of how a participant will interact with each task. Each task must be assigned a participant, and it must be determined whether that participant will be a person or a machine.

Automation, by definition, will help in this part of the analysis. Two possible extremes would be a totally automated workflow (unlikely in all but the rarest of circumstances in the graphic arts) where all participants were machines, versus a workflow with no automation where all the participants were people. In reality, almost any graphic arts workflow will involve both types of participant.

It is likely that single participants will interact with multiple tasks in the workflow. A single person may concurrently perform multiple individual tasks: page assembly, imposition, and proofing, for example. Likewise, a single machine may work on multiple tasks in the workflow; for instance, a workflow or print server could be responsible for image swapping and trapping.

The level of interaction between participant and task also needs to be established in the process. There are three possibilities for interaction: initiation, management, or performance. Initiation will normally involve a human being making decisions and providing input for a job, then allowing a machine to actually perform the task. Many software trapping applications function in exactly this manner. The operator inputs color data and desired trap geometry to the software package; the application then performs the task.

If trapping is done manually through a page-layout program like QuarkXPress, a human being will be required to perform the task in its entirety. Many tasks in a graphic arts workflow involve initiation, because although computers are excellent at crunching numbers, they are limited in their decision-making skills by the logic of their software.

In semi-automated workflows, human participants often manage the performance of tasks by machines. If a RIP is part of a workflow server. it will normally have automated procedures that handle the processing of each job, but it may require a human operator to monitor the process, assuring that each job is prioritized and directed through the correct procedures.

Verifying the participant and level of involvement is a huge help in estimating the resource potential of a workflow. Generally it can be assumed that automated tasks will require less time than managed or performed tasks. The resource potential bottlenecks will nearly always be found when jobs require high levels of human interaction, which is in large part why there has been such a large trend toward automation in the printing industry.

Managing workflow resources will require managing the human resources in the workflow. The goal is to have your employees focusing only on the tasks that absolutely require their knowledge and decision-making skills, allowing repetitive tasks to be performed by machines.

Information Resources
To accomplish a task in a workflow system, one more variable must be taken into account. Not only do the task and participant need to be defined but information resources necessary to the completion of the job must also be supplied. This can include job-related information like number of pages, number of colors, and press on which the job will be run, as well as information about the progress of the job through the workflow. A strategy must be established for supplying a participant with all needed information about the job as it relates to a particular task.

In printing, this can be especially problematic because each job carries with it a specific set of variables. There are few, if any, jobs moving through a printing plant that share all of the same characteristics. There are simply too many job-specific variables. Two jobs may both be in process color running on the same press but have completely different page geometries, impositions, and finishing requirements.

This adds two levels of complexity to information resources in printing. First, it is absolutely critical that all information be supplied correctly. Second, it limits the amount of automation that can be applied to the workflow.

In traditional workflows, job information was supplied to a participant via a job jacket, a physical folder that accompanied the job throughout its progress in the plant. The job docket, estimating information, proofs with approvals or changes, and original artwork were held in the job jacket, and employees simply rifled through it until they found the information they needed.

In a digital workflow, the job-jacket method becomes problematic because there is no physical representation of the job—it exists solely as a digital file. A valid replacement for a job jacket in a digital workflow is the use of a digital job ticket that accompanies the digital files as they move from server to workstation through the plant. All needed information about the job is either manually input at the planning or estimating stage or it can exist as a data file generated from an estimating program. Essentially the digital job ticket acts as a digital job jacket that provides the participants the information required to accomplish each task.

In reality there often are physical materials, though, that must accompany the job throughout the shop. Proofs, disks, supplied films, and original artwork are all still a part of the job. Normally we end up with a combination system. A physical job jacket is used to carry related materials, while a digital job ticket is used to feed information to scheduling and automated systems.

An additional advantage to using a structured format for digital job tickets is that many production workflow systems can be configured to read specific fields within the job ticket. The job ticket acts somewhat like a database, supplying the workflow software with needed information. This allows automation to occur in the process, with the logic being initiated by whoever inputs the data to the digital job ticket.

This level of automation can be applied throughout the workflow. It can be used to carry color and screening information to the RIP and can even link to established imposition templates. The limitations of automation are set only by the limitations of the workflow server and system being used in the shop.

Even if technology solutions are limited, it is still possible to set up job ticket–based automation using scripts. A majority of direct-to-press applications can now accept input from scripts.

Scheduling programs can be similarly configured to read information from a digital job ticket. The scheduling program logs the sequence of tasks needed to complete the job, which tasks have already been completed, where the next needed task is located, and the priority of the job. The scheduling software then compares the job ticket to its own logic instructions, sees which tasks have been completed, and routes the job appropriately.

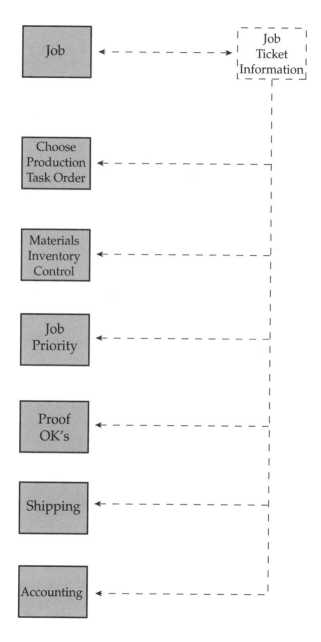

A digital job ticket can provide multiple levels of information.

The Adobe Portable Job Ticket format is a file format linked to the Adobe Acrobat PDF file format and is currently the most likely candidate for establishment as a standardized data file that can contain all needed information for workflow automation and scheduling. As the Committee for Graphic Arts Technology Standards moves closer to approval of PDF/X-1 as a valid standard for the exchange of digital art, it will be interesting to see if the Portable Job Ticket format increases in use as a standardized method for exchanging job-related information.

In addition to this standard format, there also are proprietary formats that can be used with specific workflow and scheduling systems. If you are considering the purchase of new workflow-related technology, you may wish to include the availability of digital job tickets as a consideration in the purchase.

Organizing Tasks in the Workflow
By the time you reach the point at which you are ready to organize tasks in the workflow, you should be armed with all the information you can possibly gather about how work gets done in your plant. You should know by this point, and have listed, what specific tasks need to be done in the workflow.

You should know what the participants and level of involvement will be for each task, and which information resources will be supplied to those participants. Participants can be listed as either people, equipment, or some combination. Another effective way to accomplish this is by listing participants by skill set instead of by individual. By matching needed skill sets with existing staff, you can identify new opportunities where people may be underutilized, or identify areas where training can help build efficiency.

You should also have collected data about how the existing workflow functions within your plant today. You need to know how jobs are processed through the various departments and who works at each section to get the job completed.

A solid strategy for task organization needs to begin by outlining where the problems exist in the current workflow. You are looking for bottlenecks in the process, excessive latency, and places where consistent errors are made that require rework. Do not attempt to haphazardly begin a random reorganization of tasks just to "see what will happen." Your goal is to change the workflow gradually, only where needed, with specific goals in mind. Identifying the problem areas will show you exactly where changes need to be made.

Bottlenecks in the workflow are some of the easiest problem areas to identify. A bottleneck is any point in the workflow where a task cannot be completed fast enough to keep up with the input being supplied to it. Bottlenecks are critical to the workflow because they establish the overall speed of the production system. To use a cliché, the bottleneck is the weakest link in the production chain.

Having computers with the fastest processors, or network systems that never cause delays or go down, does not actually set the overall speed for the system. We need to consider that speed is a measurement of how many jobs are produced by the entire workflow. We measure this by looking only at the end of the process. Consider it in terms of accounting. Jobs only count when they can be billed, and this only happens when the job leaves the system.

It is easy to illustrate how bottlenecks affect the overall speed of the workflow. Consider a hypothetical workflow that contains four common tasks: preflight, page assembly, proofing, and imaging. As a part of the constraints on this system, we assume that a job cannot progress to the next stage until all work is completed on the current stage. The available resources include three workstations dedicated to preflighting, four workstations dedicated to page assembly, one proofing device, and one imaging device.

In addition, we need to know the maximum production potential for each task. In this case we will say that each preflighting station can process three jobs per hour, each page-assembly station can process two jobs per hour, our proofing station can handle three jobs per hour, and our imaging device can handle five jobs per hour. If we were to diagram this workflow it would look something like the following:

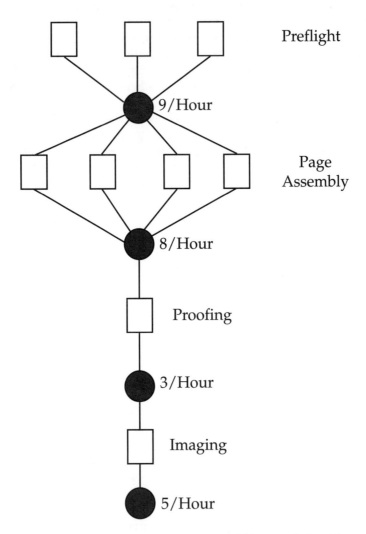

Despite all other elements, the maximum output of this system is three jobs per hour.

The value of creating diagrams for analyzing workflow is that it allows us to instantly visualize apparent problems. What happens to this system when it is operating at its maximum throughput? What is the maximum number of jobs that can be imaged in a single hour?

Though you may think that the answer is five, the production capability of the imaging device, this is incorrect. Nine jobs per hour can move into page assembly after preflighting. Of these nine jobs, eight per hour can move into proofing after page assembly. The proofer, however, can process only three of these eight jobs each hour.

How many jobs can be imaged each hour? Despite the potential of the device to produce five jobs per hour, only three jobs per hour, the maximum speed of the proofer, will be actually be imaged. The total output of the workflow, defined here as number of jobs imaged, is set by the slowest task in the workflow—the proofer.

When this system is functioning with maximum input, what will happen to the jobs? They will continue to back up at the proofing stage of the workflow. Eventually there will be a large collection of jobs sitting idle waiting to be proofed, while at the same time the imaging device will often be standing idle waiting for jobs to be supplied to it.

Identifying these situations is akin to identifying latency. Job latency occurs anytime a job sits idle in a printing plant and no work is being done to it. Some latency is unavoidable in the production workflow. This is the reason why we created the logic block "hold for approval" in the previous chapter. To identify excessive latency in the workflow, we are looking for situations where jobs are incurring latency time at points where they should actually be moving through the workflow. There is a direct relationship between production bottlenecks and job latency. Find a bottleneck, and you will find latency.

The reverse can often work as well: Find latency, and you have potentially identified a bottleneck. This gives us an excellent tool for discovering where bottlenecks occur in the process. One of the best strategies is to create a method whereby the time it takes to complete each task in the workflow is measured. If areas are found where jobs continually take longer to be processed than they should, that is a likely place to begin looking for a bottleneck.

Identifying areas where excessive errors requiring remakes occur should be relatively easy. If a proof returns with errors track where the error occurred. For example, a type reflow error (a problem that can occur frequently with digital fonts) may be attributed to the page assembly stage of the workflow. Consistent type errors would indicate inefficiency with this particular task in the workflow.

Once tasks that cause errors have been identified, it may take further work to get to the root cause of the problem—type reflowing is often caused by incorrect file-management strategies. However, identifying the particular task involved is a necessary first step in beginning the process of further identifying the root cause of the problem.

Measurement and Indicators

It should be apparent by now that finding the problem areas in a workflow system requires consistent measurement and analysis. The success of workflow problem solving will be directly affected by how well the workflow is measured and how well the resultant data is analyzed. A sound strategy for measurement needs to include valid assumptions of what will be measured, how it will be measured, and how the data will be analyzed.

The first thing to identify is exactly what will be measured. There are many things that can be measured in a production environment; what needs to be discovered are a few critical items that will act as a pulse of the workflow. These items are called key indicators; they are crucial, finite, and measurable areas that point out problems occurring in the process. Though most key indicators are different for each company, there are some that can generically be applied to virtually any printing company. Plate remakes are an excellent example of a key indicator that is easily measurable and will instantly point out problems in the production process.

There must also be a plan for how each key indicator will be measured. Plate remakes, for example, could be measured as a straight number per month. But because of volume changes, this would be a relatively useless number. The same key indicator could also be approached as a percentage of remakes to the total number of plates made. Taking this measurement as a percentage accounts for volume changes and is much more useful in determining problems in the process.

Finally, you must determine what you will be measuring your key indicators against. Usually, key indicators are benchmarked against some industry standards that represent the production levels of the best companies in the industry. In the printing industry, these numbers are available as the PIA (Printing Industries of America) Ratios. The PIA Ratios are a carefully compiled list made from surveys sent to thousands of printing companies in the United States.

Your local or state trade association may also offer a similar service, but the PIA Ratios are recognized as the best source of accurate benchmarking figures. Benchmarking figures can also be an excellent starting point for identifying key indicators within your own company.

Allocating Resources To Match Production Flow
If you look back at the hypothetical workflow we created for bottleneck analysis, you will notice there seem to be problems in moving jobs from preflight through page assembly. At maximum production, one extra job per hour is produced by preflight that cannot be processed in time at the page-assembly stage. The reason this was not immediately identified as a bottleneck has to do with the irregular flow of jobs through the workflow.

Production work often seems to come in to printing companies in a "feast or famine" method; there are either too many jobs or not enough jobs coming into the plant at one time. In reality, the workflow will not always be strained by having to perform at maximum potential. There will always be some busy times and some slow times. Resources in the workflow should be flexible enough so that they can be allocated as needed to accommodate this natural ebb and flow of business.

In the previous example, we allocated three workstations for preflight and four for page assembly. But there is no reason why these workstations cannot be assigned to other tasks if production levels dictate it. One of the advantages of working with desktop computers in production is that they can perform multiple tasks depending solely on which software applications are used. Consider what would happen if one of the preflight stations was configured and staffed so that it could be used for page assembly if required.

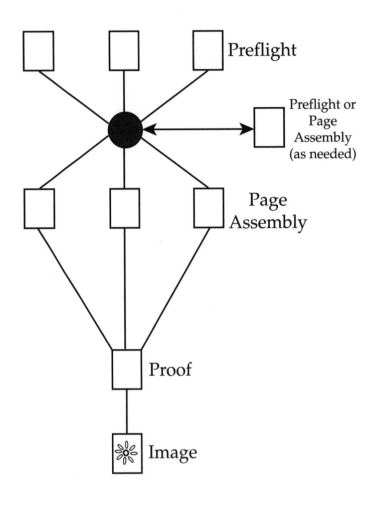

Systems should be flexible to accommodate slow and busy times at the plant.

By reorganizing the allocation of resources to the workflow, the system is now flexible enough to accommodate busy and slow times in the production cycle. This is common practice that can be easily implemented not only for preflight and page assembly but can also include imposition stations if that task is performed using standardized desktop software.

Some companies have also found it beneficial to keep old computers available for use to help out during peak business times. Though they may be too slow for day-to-day use, it might be just enough extra processing power to get jobs through in a timely fashion on a busy day. Be aware that this also has staffing implications. The skill set required for page assembly is more advanced than that of preflighting.

Correction Cycles
Frequently, jobs within the production cycle will need to return through a single task or set of tasks to accommodate changes that are made to the content or page geometry. These correction cycles must be expected and accounted for in the workflow and are frequently initiated as a result of internal quality-control checks.

Correction cycles can be triggered through external decisions about the job, as well—for example, if the designer has made a typographic mistake or if content within the document needs to be updated. In these cases, called author alterations, there needs to be financial accountability as well. Some companies lose thousands of dollars each year by failing to bill for changes to work that were initiated by the customer. Businesses do not grow by giving away work for free.

An effective quality-control procedure should include the option of returning a job for corrections. One of the added benefits of workflow analysis and restructuring is that it provides a company with the opportunity to measure errors in their process, and thus locate and solve the causes of those errors. It is wise to perform internal checks of the process before proofs are sent out for customer approval. Catching an error before the customer does can help to prevent cycle time and scheduling delays.

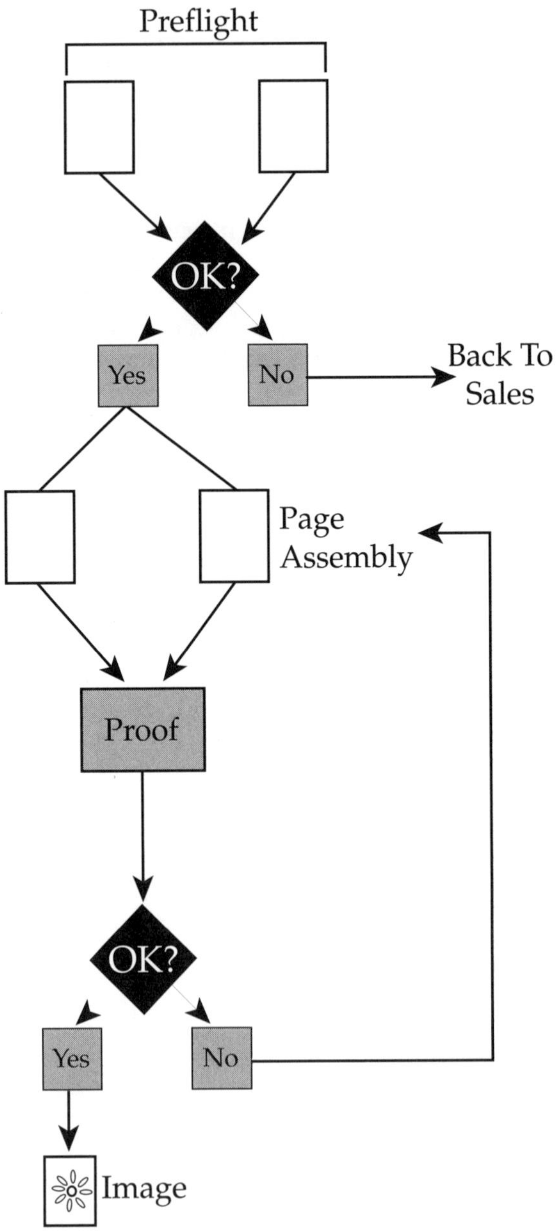

Preflight

OK?

Yes

No

Back To
Sales

Page
Assembly

Proof

OK?

Yes

No

Image

Correction cycles account for needed changes to a job.

Note that in each case some decision must be made whether the job will enter a correction cycle. There are numerous strategies that can be employed for the authority to make this decision. Some companies require a supervisor or manager to approve jobs at certain points before they are allowed to progress further.

An approach that follows more modern management practices, however, is to allow employees to verify their own work by including quality control as a part of the task procedures. This approach involves the entire company in the quality program, and adds the benefit of empowering employees by giving them some level of self-management.

Even if all sources of internal error were to be removed, the allowance of correction cycles would still be required to accommodate changes made by the customer. Though customer changes, unlike internally triggered corrections, can be billed to the client, it is still best to avoid this sequence where possible. The effect of corrections on scheduling often negates any dollar amount that can be charged for author alterations.

Involving the creative task as a part of the production workflow, through communications and feedback with the customer, can often help to minimize many of the common errors that are found to require corrections.

When the printing company begins to accept making these changes without making any attempt to motivate the designer to produce problem-free work, it takes on the role of designer. Though some may argue that this provides a new revenue stream to the printing company, this is not really the case.

Printing companies are, first and foremost, manufacturers of products. Profit opportunity in a printing company comes primarily from the cylinders turning on the most expensive pieces of equipment in the plant: the printing presses. Any distractions or delays in moving work toward the press actually decrease profitability. The rule of thumb is that if cylinders are not turning, the company is not making money.

One of the advantages to integrated workflow systems is their ability to impose post-RIPed files by using a RIP Once—Output Many or Normalize Once—Raasterize Many approach. Though this will not help prevent errors, which is by far the best goal, it will help to minimize the time and cost involved with correcting, assembling, and imaging files. This is one of the main advantages to using systems that support late binding changes.

Chapter 17

Automation in the Workflow

One of the key goals in increasing workflow efficiency is the creation of automation within the system for commonly repeated sets of tasks. As the workflow is assessed it will become clear that certain subsets within the workflow are performed on every job that comes through the shop.

Automating these task sets allows employees to focus their attention on the more important decision-dependent sections of the workflow, while taking a monitoring role over systems that have been established to handle iterative tasks.

No matter how careful or experienced the employee, we must be aware that even in performing simple repetitive tasks people will make mistakes. One of the benefits to automation is that it removes the "human" factor from these operations. With labor being the largest source of cost after paper within the printing plant, it is essential that resources be structured to provide maximum benefit from human resources where needed, rather than squandering them in repetitive tasks.

The difficulty in automating tasks within the graphic arts workflow is that each job has slightly different characteristics. We need to differentiate between job-specific characteristics and workflow-specific characteristics. The argument that automation is impossible because each job is different considers only the printed piece and ignores the fact that the steps required to perform each job are very similar.

The simplest example might be in the production of two sixteen-page saddle-stitched booklets that differ in colors and paper but share the same binding style and trim size. One job may require scans that need to be proofed and placed, while the other has all components included. Despite the differences in the job specifications, the similarities in binding and trim mean that we can use templates for imposition and proofing. Automation is based on looking for similarities from job to job.

Automation in Closed Production Cycles

Different types of production systems require different approaches to automation in the workflow. We have to differentiate between closed and open production systems. In a closed-loop system all work is done within the printing company in the preparation of a job. Scans, type preparation, page layout, and then the standard prepress production tasks of imposition, proofing, and platemaking all occur within a single company. A newspaper might typically fall into this category of business, in essence maintaining ownership of the job from start to finish.

Closed-cycle systems have an advantage in automation because a single company controls all aspects of the job production, and all production is done on a known set of equipment. Characterizations are easy to develop because all input sources can be precisely defined for each job.

One of the more difficult tasks to automate is color control. This is necessary to account for specific characteristics in the final printing system. Images destined, for example, for a gravure press must be treated differently from images destined for offset lithography to achieve optimal reproduction. Closed-cycle systems have an advantage in automating color correction because all input sources can be identified and specific workflows established for each set.

The use of multiple parallel workflows for color correction is often found in newspapers. Many newspapers have begun or have already moved to digital cameras because it removes the need for generating photographic film—imperative in this deadline-critical environment. Nonetheless, images are often still submitted as chromes or prints from freelance photographers or other sources.

A typical approach to automating this type of system involves both automated and manual parallel workflows. The digital cameras that will be used by the in-house photographers are characterized according to their color-reproduction qualities. Scripts driving image-editing software, or a color-management system, can then be set up in combination with a set of hot folders to automatically optimize each image. In parallel, images from freelance or other outside sources follow a different workflow path through the company so that each can be scanned and manually corrected.

Another advantage in closed systems comes from the ability to use standard templates for page layout and assembly. One of the stumbling blocks to workflow efficiency often comes at the page-assembly stage of prepress as jobs need to be converted from standard reader spreads into a printable format. The difficulty is not so much in the layout of individual pages, which is handled easily by imposition programs, but in the alteration of page geometries, which designers may be unaware of. When all work is kept in-house, it becomes possible to set up standard templates for each type of job and then flow text within those templates.

Automation in Open Production Cycles

Open production systems are much more common in the commercial printing industry, and likewise much more difficult to automate. In an open system, files are submitted from a variety of sources. A job may include electronic illustrations, stock photo images, previously archived images, and scanned images from different sources, all combined into a single document. As the number of sources increases, it becomes difficult to accurately characterize all of the devices in the production chain.

Automating an open system frequently takes place after manual adjustment and verification of digital files. Whereas in a closed system color control can be automated because the input variables are known, in an open system there must be some human interaction; the variables are simply too excessive to accurately program an automated system to account for.

Accurate preflighting—verifying that all files needed for a job are present before allowing it to enter the production cycle—becomes the most critical part of the automation procedure in an open system. Preflighting ensures that the incoming "raw materials" for print manufacturing—text, images, illustrations, and layouts—conform to the requirements of the system. Verifying that all incoming materials conform to a particular specification gives us the basic information we need to consider automation further downstream in the workflow.

Preflighting generally falls into two levels. The first level takes place as soon as a job enters the printing company, often before the job is estimated. It verifies that all needed files, images, illustrations, and fonts are included and are at the appropriate resolutions. Often a customer service representative or the salesperson can be trained to perform these sorts of early preflights. Software packages are available that will even read the appropriate layout files and generate a printed report indicating whether the job passes or fails the preflight test.

The second level of preflight is used to verify that files meet the specific printing characteristics, most often for color accuracy. Often this level of preflighting is combined with the page-assembly stage of production because excellent technical skills are needed by the operator to verify that files have been correctly adjusted for gray balance, dot gain, and other system-specific characteristics.

Because these characteristics will always be slightly different from shop to shop, and even between different presses within a single shop, human intervention is needed to perform this check. Once it has been determined that the files and layout for a job meet the predetermined specifications, the files can be entered into a system designed to automate production tasks like imposition, image swapping, and proofing.

Automating Color
Recently, color-management systems have been receiving more and more attention as a strategy for automating color reproduction. Color-management systems work by building color look-up tables for a scanner, monitor, or press/printer. By knowing the specific reproduction characteristics of two devices, color management provides an automated link between the two color spaces that

optimize an image for reproduction without the need for human interaction (beyond, of course, characterizing the devices).

In theory, by characterizing each device in the chain, it should be possible to automate all of the tasks related to the color reproduction of images. In reality, however, many users are finding that this noble goal cannot be realized in all situations. Open production systems are particularly difficult to automate using color management because it becomes nearly impossible to characterize every single input source.

The difficulty comes not only from the large number of sources but also from the fact that some knowledge of colorimetry and the possession of a spectrophotometer at the design stage are necessary to integrate these systems.

The issue becomes one more of accountability than technology. For color management to work, systems must be constantly calibrated and maintained. The question that seems to be unanswered is how to verify the state of calibration for a piece of equipment at another site. For example, if a designer is sending color-managed RGB files to a printer, both the designer's and the printer's systems must be perfectly calibrated for accurate color to result.

If $1,000 of bad film is generated, who is accountable for the cost? The reason that traditional methods for manual color verification work is that they provide a needed level of accountability and responsibility required for printing.

Another problematic issue for color management is that it cannot automatically make the adjustments needed for different image types. Images generally fall into three categories. Hi-key images are overall very bright: a woman in a wedding dress standing against a white wall. Low-key images are overall very dark: a black cat in a coal bin. Normal-key images have tones that are relatively evenly distributed across the scale.

Color management works well for normal-key images, but hi-key or low-key images require special contrast adjustments to reproduce correctly. Color management is simply not "smart" enough to recognize the type of image and make the appropriate adjustments. Yet another issue surrounding color management is in detail enhancement. Digitized images must be artificially sharpened to match the original when printed. Called "unsharp masking," this involves creating artificial high-contrast areas within specific tonal regions of the image. Correct detail enhancement depends on the content of the image and must be assessed individually for each image. Color-management systems are unable to make this adjustment.

An excellent workaround for these problems seems to be in the use of hybrid systems—using color management in conjunction with some operator decisions. In this model, an operator scans an image to an RGB file using generic color settings for a scanner. They can then open the file and perform detail enhancement, as well as manually adjusting for the "keyness" of the image.

Once these adjustments have been made, the file can be converted to CMYK for printing, using color management. This process can yield excellent results, and though it does not fully automate image reproduction, it does allow the computer to automatically take into account any inherent color-reproduction issues that exist with the devices themselves.

Another area where color management shows promise is in digital proofing. Though the intent of proofing is to predict the final outcome of a job, no proofing device inherently matches specific press conditions. This means that color data for the proofer must be altered so that the resulting proof can match a standard press sheet. Color management does exactly this type of conversion.

Many RIPs have the ability to accept either ICC standard profiles or specific color-rendering dictionaries (CRDs). Incoming color data is then sent through these look-up tables and altered before being imaged. Some RIPs even have the ability to apply different types of rendering to different types of objects to enhance color matching. Images, for example, might be tagged for perceptual rendering while text or screen-built CMYK solids are tagged for colorimetric rendering.

Though color management may not currently provide end-to-end automation for color reproduction in all cases, there are still many opportunities where it can be useful. It should be remembered that color management is still a very young technology based on a sound concept. It is likely that as the technology matures, color management will have more viability in its application to print production.

Automation in Document Management

Typically, strategies for document management are used to control the creation of documents in a networked environment where multiple participants are involved in the process. In such a system it becomes necessary to place controls on the document structure so that users can verify that they are working on the correct section of a job stored on a single main server.

For example, there may be different people tasked to produce text content, illustrations, and final layout for a document. If a central server is used to contain the job, the illustrator must know whether the current version of the document is ready for illustration before they begin. If the illustrator bases work on incomplete text, then time will be wasted in the creation of the document. Each participant must know the current status of the job for this creation strategy to be successful.

Because participants in the process may have no contact with each other, and in fact may be located in different geographic areas, the complexity lies in assuring that participants are given the correct information to work with. Document management normally takes one of two possible approaches: versioning or a check-in/checkout system, or some combination of the two.

Though not every aspect of document management can be directly applied to print production, many of the same problems exist from the similar server-client environment. As jobs are passed from task to task through various participants, some strategy is required to assure that each participant is working on the correct version of the job. It is also necessary to tag the job so that as actions are performed, the status of the job can be verified.

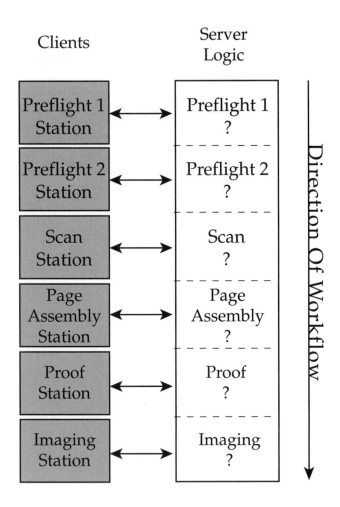

Process logic within the server can route jobs through the system as needed.

For instance, we can assume a job must go through the following set of tasks: preflight I, preflight II, scanning, page assembly, proofing, and imaging. Each task requires that the previous task has been completed. If the page assembly takes place before preflight II, the process logic of the workflow has been broken, and problems will inevitably occur.

Tracking these changes requires implementing some system for versioning. The simplest method might be to just save a new version of each file as it progresses through the shop. A simple suffix attached to the file name would be sufficient to inform each participant of the current job status. Though this accomplishes the goal of verifying job status, it does not place automation into the system.

For automation to occur, the status-verification system must be tied into some outside logic process that helps to move the job through the shop. A complex system would not only account for the status of the job but would also send the appropriate files to the next needed task. Advanced scheduling systems take advantage of this type of logic. As each participant finishes or task is completed, the file is marked as okay to go on to the next stage of the process.

These systems can also be helpful by taking the urgency of each job into account. Jobs marked "urgent" will be automatically routed to the top of the queue for processing at each station. Another advantage is the ability of the system to constantly maintain a current scheduling database that can be accessed not only within the plant but, via some Web or other Internet connection, be made directly available to the client. This completely integrated system both controls the movement of the job through the workflow and acts as a reporting system so scheduling efficiency can be increased.

Scripts
Scripts can be extremely powerful tools in automating repetitive tasks within the production workflow. A scripting language is similar to a programming language but is used to control the operating system or scriptable applications. Scripts can be used to perform tasks on sets of files within a folder, either performing system-based tasks or controlling other applications to perform tasks on files.

One of the advantages to scripts is that they are quite easy to learn. Though they do require a small bit of programming skills to create, they are nowhere near as complex as high-level languages like C++.

Scripts can be used only in combination with applications that can accept commands from them, called scriptable applications. This means that the program can be controlled by action commands that are given in the script. Fortunately, most of the common applications used in prepress production are scriptable, which means they can be controlled via external scripts.

An example is helpful in understanding how scripts work. Suppose that there is a RIP within the production system that cannot accept files using the underscore character (_) within a file name. Solving this problem requires that as each job enters the workflow, files using this character need to be identified and the offending character removed from the file name. Preferably this should happen as part of the preflight procedure.

Without scripts, a person would be required to spend time on each job going through all files looking for the underscore character, a highly repetitive task that begs for automation. Using scripts, it is possible to write a procedure that will automatically identify any such file. By activating the script and pointing it to a particular folder, the script will automatically identify the nonconformant file, which can then be renamed. Not only does this automate the process, it also will remove the files that will inevitably slip through due to human error.

An interesting application for scripts is in concert with color management. ColorSync, the operating system–level color-management system that comes with Macintosh computers, is fully scriptable. If a color-management system is in place at a company, it is possible to place a large number of files into a single location, activate a script, and then walk away while the computer automatically performs RGB to CMYK transformations.

Though the basics of writing scripts are beyond the scope of this book, there are many excellent texts available for self-teaching scripting languages, both for experienced programmers or novice users.

Hot Folders

A hot folder is a directory that moves a file immediately into a specific task. Hot-folder options are often included as a part of proprietary systems but can also be created in open systems through the use of scripts. Like scripts, hot folders can be an extremely powerful tool in automating production workflows.

Hot folders often act in an automated network transfer. A hot folder might be set up on the desktop of a workstation that leads directly to a proofer queue. The operator creates a valid file type for the proofer, usually PostScript, TIFF, or PDF, and then drags the file into the appropriate hot folder. The file is then automatically routed to the proofer where it can be imaged immediately or held so that it can be ganged with other images on a single sheet to conserve materials. Dragging the file into the hot folder replaces the repetitive task of choosing a specific printer, connecting across the network, and then printing the file to the appropriate printer.

Another type of hot folder is known as a watched folder. In a watched-folder system, an application is directed to constantly check a specific folder at certain time intervals. If a new file is found in the watched folder, the application is launched and a set of actions is performed on the file. Adobe Acrobat Distiller, used to create PDF files from PostScript files, is just one of many applications that have the ability to use watched folders.

Often a combination of hot folders with watched folders can be used to speed the workflow. An example of such a case can be found in PDF workflows where files are converted to PDF before they are sent to the RIP. The user could set up a watched folder called "incoming PostScript" and a hot folder connected to the RIP called "outgoing PDF" on their desktop. Distiller could then be directed to convert files in the watched folder to PDF and automatically save them to the hot folder. The result saves an enormous amount of operator time needed to open, convert, save, and copy files by hand. Watched/hot folders are an important part of automated workflow.

Hot Folders on Desktop

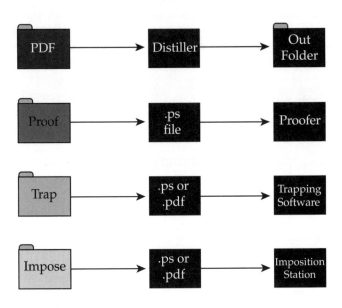

Hot folders can help provide automation and save time.

Templates

Using predefined templates is another very simple method of adding automation to the workflow. Templates are particularly helpful in digital imposition and page-layout applications where many jobs follow the same format. In fact, most page-layout and imposition programs have the ability to use predefined templates built in to their software.

Page-layout programs can be set up not only with single templates but can also use multiple page templates, called master pages, within a single document. Company newsletters or direct-mail pieces that are produced on a regular basis with different content but the same layout are prime candidates for the use of page layout templates. Headers, footers, mastheads, or other elements that remain consistent from document to document can all be set up within these templates.

Imposition templates are useful when multiple jobs use the same trim size and binding style. Content is irrelevant in these cases unless a special case forces a change in the imposition. Book production is an excellent example of the usefulness of imposition templates. Most printing companies already use some form of imposition template in the planning stage of the job. Taking the time to convert these paper layouts into digital templates is a relatively simple task that will save a large amount of time.

Automating Archiving and Backup
Any archiving and backup software used should have the ability for automation built in to the software. Automating these tasks is important not only to create efficiency but also to ensure that these tasks are performed on a regular basis. Unfortunately, it is often unwise to rely on a person to perform this critical task.

How automation is applied to archiving and backup depends on the exact system set up at your location as well as the specific type of software used to perform these tasks. Automation can be as simple as specifying a time to copy files to some external media, or as complex as creating specific network connections to other workstations and controlling the type of media where the backup will be saved. Many archiving systems can even be set up to shut down workstations after the task has been completed.

Archiving and backup should be set to occur at off-peak times, especially if files will need to be copied across a network. This will avoid degrading performance of the workstations and the network as backup is performed.

Automation in Proprietary Workflow Systems
One of the main advantages in purchasing a specific workflow system from a vendor is the support for automation built into the system. Though scripts, hot folders, and templates are valuable tools, it is difficult to match the sophistication of a unified workflow

system. Developers often include automated hot folders within their system that can be customized for a variety of uses within the workflow.

Not only are the connections to these systems automated, they also apply automation within the processing engines themselves. Most major systems can be customized so that specific workflows themselves can be created within the system. These processes can redirect files to specific proofing systems, change file resolutions as needed for different devices, offer automated trapping solutions, allow for on-screen preview of files , and offer advanced imposition strategies. With all these pieces adding automation to the process, using one of these systems can add a tremendous amount of efficiency to the workflow.

If automation is critical to your workflow, you should consider purchasing a workflow system. Though they can be costly, no other strategy offers the ease of setup and use found in these systems.

Chapter 18

Workflow and Process Management

As a company begins to evaluate its workflow system, strengths and weaknesses of the current system become evident. In a migration to a digital workflow, the changes that need to be made are often so extensive that it is necessary to reevaluate the entire business process model so that the new workflow can be integrated.

Workflow adjustments allow a company to find new ways to make use of human and technical resources, to streamline the production process, and to meet customer demands. A valuable benefit to workflow reengineering is to open opportunities to adjusting the entire process.

A digital workflow cannot be viewed as merely existing within the production line. Digital becomes an end-to-end process. Where does the digital workflow begin? Often it starts the first time a sales representative contacts a potential customer or gives the customer specifications for correctly submitting files to the printer. The customer's creative work sets the beginning for a digital workflow. Where does the digital workflow end? Not until the job has been delivered and permanently archived.

Between these two points, the digital workflow must accommodate color management, materials handling, accounting costs—in short, everything concerning that job. Correctly moving to a digital workflow is an all-inclusive process.

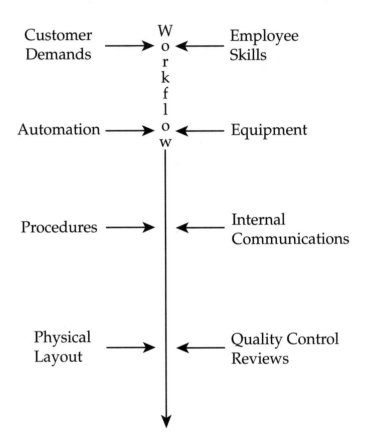

Your workflow is affected by many variables throughout the process.

Business Environment
The environment in which a printer operates affects the workflow by setting the method in which customer needs will be satisfied. The business environment is really what sets the need for making any changes at all to the workflow. If the workflow already met the needs of the environment, there would be no reason to make any changes. The workflow must address issues of competition in the marketplace, turnaround requirements, quality requirements, the type of customer being serviced, and flexibility to customers' demands.

Workflow has a tremendous effect on a company's ability to be competitive within its market. This is aggravated by the fact that it has become increasingly difficult to differentiate between value services of different printing companies. Many print buyers may have multiple printers within their area that all have essentially the same equipment. Depending on how technologically savvy the print buyers are, they see no real difference between two companies that both offer six-color Heidelberg presses with similar bindery operations. The effect has been to drive pricing of jobs to a commodity level.

Workflow allows a company to add value differentiation to its process by streamlining production and removing errors that slow cycle times and degrade customer confidence in the printer. A company that can consistently meet scheduling requirements has more value to a print buyer than one that is struggling to avoid delays in production. Effective preflighting in the workflow increases confidence by allowing more accurate estimates and identifying errors early in the process. Discovering that a font is missing three days after a customer has supplied a file to you will inevitably force the customer to wonder why there is a lack of organization within the printing company.

An effective workflow allows a printing company to be flexible to customer demands. This can involve issues of archiving, changes, and scheduling. Responsiveness is based on the ability of the printer to quickly locate a customer's job, whether prior work or work in progress, and offer feedback as needed. This depends on the document-management strategy used within the company. Some numeric sequence or system for cataloging jobs should be enabled so that computer searches will be accurate. Attempting to locate a customer's job by searching for the text string "new layout" will, for obvious reasons, be completely ineffective.

The document-management system should use numeric identification tags that cross departments. A financial question about job 999999 should be able to generate a report that includes information about the current status, whether that be a location within the workflow or on some archived media. The sharpest of these systems allow customers to interactively inquire about their jobs via some telecommunications link. Systems can be created where the customer interfaces with the printer's network through a World Wide Web site.

As a part of the workflow system, customer changes must be accounted for. Not only must the change be accepted, made, and verified, the system should also have the capability of assessing or accepting the cost for these changes. It is often overlooked that many printers lose thousands of dollars each year in unbilled authors' alterations. Accounting for this up front in the workflow is one way to directly add dollars to the company as a result of the workflow reengineering.

Meeting a customer's quality needs requires some definition of the inherently vague term "quality." The best way to define a job as quality is in terms of meeting a customer's overall needs. If a customer is not picky about color but needs the job tomorrow, no amount of high-end color editing is going to make that job high quality. Only delivering the job on time will satisfy that customer's perception of quality. Workflow changes help meet quality requirements by allowing the system to be flexible to meet whatever need is posed to the printer.

Changing the Manufacturing Process

Traditional graphic arts workflows followed a model of fragmentation manufacturing. Each task in the process was removed yet dependent on the task that immediately preceded it. It was very similar to building a car, where individual components are created and then the components are assembled via some type of assembly line. In the graphic arts, raw materials of ideas and layouts are used instead of steel and plastic, but the essential concept is the same.

The management strategies for supervising this assembly-line process involved a series of middle managers who were responsible for micromanaging their particular section of the process but who had little view of the overall breadth of the process. Frequently, tasks were not even within the same location; typesetting, separations, and platemaking could take place within three entirely different companies. The effect was a system overburdened with management and short of communications.

Digital workflows require a more modern approach to manufacturing in order to be effective. Parallel processes mean that management must be aware of the entirety of each project. For instance, a designer may still be creating the final digital mechanical while another company is providing the color separations—in digital format, of course.

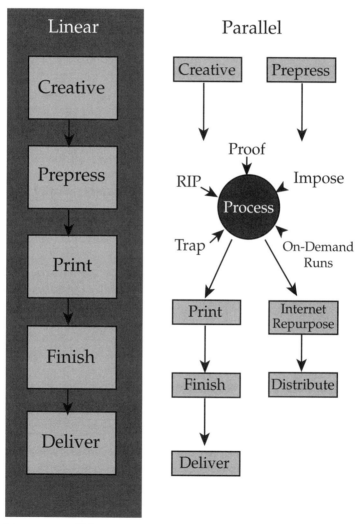

Linear vs. parallel processes.

The push toward operating in a parallel process comes both from management and new technology. Companies are finding that removing middle management and letting the production team focus on the overall process, rather than only a single section, increases communications and understanding within the company. Employees are urged to view their downstream associates as customers rather than competitors.

Communication increases not only between employees but also from the company to the client. As the employees learn more about the overall process, they are better equipped to handle customer questions and changes flexibly and responsively.

Many companies are manifesting this change in management style through the creation of production teams. A team might include a production planner, customer service rep, and digital technician. Instead of handing the job off between discrete departments, the team manages the job from preflight through platemaking. Each member is aware of the job requirements and current problems.

Creating production teams as a self-management system puts responsibility and motivation back onto the shoulders of the employees themselves. At issue is the discrepancy between responsibility and authority in the production process. Through self-management, employees are empowered with the ability to have control of their day-to-day work processes. This far exceeds systems in which employees are given the responsibility for accomplishing work but the authority and means to make needed changes to the process is placed in the hands of a discrete manager.

Once employee morale has been improved and employees realize that they have the responsibility for managing themselves, an appropriate reward system should be developed within the company. The intent is to set up a system of healthy competition between teams so that results translate directly into rewards, while at the same time a spirit of shared information can be nurtured across the entire production system. The pitfall to avoid, of course, is when competitiveness becomes counterproductive as teams attempt to consistently win without regard for the overall process.

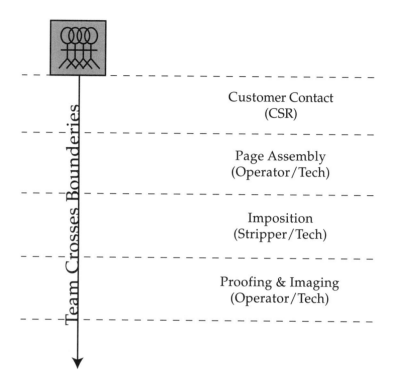

A team approach facilitates communications by removing barriers.

Technology advances, particularly with full workflow systems, also have facilitated the ability to approach production as a series of parallel processes. Many systems have the ability to concurrently RIP, trap, and impose pages as they are completed in page assembly. In the past, a 120-page piece may have had to wait in production while a single advertisement was being prepared.

The new systems allow the work to continue on unaffected pages if there is a delay somewhere in the process. The ability to impose pre-RIPed files, known as late-binding systems, also easily accommodates customer changes. A change on one page merely requires that the one page be re-RIPed rather than the entire form.

Document management should also be built directly into the client-server system. Tasks should be routed with a minimum number of handoffs. Systems should be developed that require instructions be entered only once. The estimating task is the obvious choice for entering job instructions, as all components of the process must be accounted for to accurately provide a cost structure for the job.

Combining new technical and human-resources strategies moves a company from a fragmented to an integrated production system. Employees are given the responsibility for controlling their own work and are given the technical tools and training to make this possible. This can be considered combining the thinking process with the doing process.

This has become even more of a necessity within the graphic arts as the number of employees required to complete the process shrinks but the skill set for each employee increases. Printing and publishing jobs now fall into the realm of technical expertise. Maintaining the employees who are capable of critical thinking that can effectively function in this environment requires management to consider everyone as equals within the company team itself. Change is required at every level.

Key Workflow Indicators

In any system, we need some form of metrics through which we can measure the relative success or failure of our efforts. For example, we might use a measurement like the ratio of plate remakes to total plates made to verify the consistency of the overall prepress function. In fragmented manufacturing, it was relatively easy to create these metrics because there were precise lines differentiating each task in the overall process.

In an integrated manufacturing environment, we must be more creative in our establishment of indicators to measure the process. Though we can still use precise measurements to gauge the output of the process, it is necessary to widen the scope of the metrics in order to measure the success of the entire system. Are we making the most effective use of all our human resources? As new technologies are integrated, these systems often (and should) replace formerly redundant tasks performed by employees. When this happens, a decision must be made about what to do with employees whose jobs are being displaced. Though the tasks performed by those employees may disappear, their knowledge and input to the process is still invaluable.

A common example is the relationship between strippers and digital imposition systems. Companies have found that although using digital imposition systems results in the need for fewer strippers on staff, the knowledge base owned by those employees is critical to problem solving within the process. Rather than firing the displaced employees, strippers have been moved upstream in the process to production planning. Their hands-on knowledge of the production process is now used in the planning and estimating stage of the cycle to predict problems before they can occur at a more costly downstream area.

Are we making the most effective use of our technical resources? Many companies have invested in costly workflow systems but fail to take full advantage of all the features. This usually happens because of a failure to recognize the value in taking extra time away from production to plan the overall system, or a failure to recognize or understand the full functionality of the workflow system. Features such as in-RIP trapping or color separations must be tested in the workflow in order to be utilized on a day-to-day basis.

Streamlining the workflow requires taking the necessary time to assess the full capabilities of a technical system by establishing a series of tests. Though the testing system may initially take time away from production work, it is essential to establishing a global all-inclusive plan for streamlining the production environment.

Is there a system of internal quality control? Employees should, as much as possible, be self-regulating. People need to be in control of their own process rather than managed by some outside source. This removes the cost of outside regulation and at the same time places responsibility where it belongs: in the hands of the person producing the work. Scanning and color correction provide a good example of a self-regulating quality-control system. Often companies rely on the CSR or sales rep to assure the quality of color separations before they are allowed to continue through the production process. This often means that individuals who are unfamiliar with the technical limits and processes are making integral decisions as to what is or is not acceptable. A better strategy is to put this approval process into the hands of the employee responsible for producing the work. Though this may mean initial changes in how customer needs are communicated into the system, it will be offset by the effects of reduced handoffs and approval times.

Are there minimal handoffs in the production process? Every time a job is passed to a new person, time is wasted as the new participant must become familiarized with the particular problems of that job. Most human errors that occur in the system happen because of a communications error in a handoff. Handoffs need to be reduced within a workflow system.

The use of desktop computer technology gives us an opportunity to reduce most handoffs within a digital workflow by combining tasks within a single employee and system. There is no reason why a digital job should ever be handed off to another employee as it moves through tasks that will be performed on desktop systems. This includes secondary preflight, page assembly, PostScripting, and imposition. Providing the tools and the training to each employee to perform all of these tasks in line on the same station is a better strategy for removing errors and increasing accountability in terms of job ownership. Is there adequate communication across the production workflow? Everyone involved in the workflow needs to have an understanding of the entire process. The CSR must have enough information to answer customer requests and needs. The production technician must have a clear understanding of those requests to produce the job to a customer's satisfaction.

Communication is enhanced by building organization around the entire process rather than merely focusing on a single section of the workflow. The intent is to avoid creating barriers of responsibility in employees' minds. We want them to realize that their responsibility for the success or failure of the job through the workflow is synonymous with the company's responsibility, and that by communicating across previously inviolable lines, they facilitate the entire process.

Chapter 19

Identifying and Tracking Workflow

At some point we have to roll up our sleeves and begin to map out our workflow. Creating a graphical representation of workflow is critical to identifying areas that need improvement and areas that are already performing adequately. To accomplish this, we need to have some graphical tools available to us, we need to define the scope and depth of our work, and we need to be aware of the different effects and viewpoints to look at workflows.

Workflow Tools
Almost everyone has seen a flowchart: symbols that represent different types of processes with a connecting structure that shows hierarchical relationships between each segment. Mapping workflows requires the same set of tools and can be accomplished with four basic icons: tasks, procedures, reviews, and decisions. By combining these four elements, we can outline any process within the production cycle.

Task icon

The task icon is used to represent a job or action that takes place within the workflow. The task should be a finite action performed independently of other actions. Preflighting, scanning, trapping, and imposition are examples of tasks within a digital workflow. Combining different tasks lets us view the logic of the entire process.

Procedure icon

A procedure represents fundamental actions that are required to perform a task. For instance, preflighting would involve locating the customer's files, copying them to a server, loading fonts, and checking the file for accuracy. Looking at the procedures will allow us to create or streamline the standard operating procedures for each task.

Review icon

A review occurs whenever a procedure or task needs to be checked for accuracy. Normally, a review is part of some quality-control system. Workflows require reviews to verify the accuracy of preceding procedures and tasks before allowing work to continue downstream through the system.

Decision icon

At many points along the workflow, decisions must be made both within tasks and within the entire process. Decisions always follow review steps, which verify the accuracy of work. There are three potential directions from any decision step: yes, no, or return. Each different decision initiates a discrete set of new tasks or procedures. A return decision is a special case that moves the job back to the prior step within the workflow.

It's important to distinguish exactly how to differentiate between a task and a procedure using this set of tools. Remember that we make a difference between task logic and process logic. Task logic involves establishing the specific procedures to get a single item accomplished within the workflow. Using these tools, we can map the procedures required to place high-resolution files into a page-layout document.

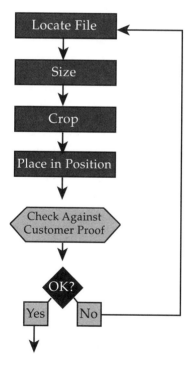

A basic workflow map to place hi-res files with correction cycle.

Notice in the preceding example the repetitive nature of the decision structure. This is a common occurrence in workflows when we need to set up a "do until" logic structure. Another common case for using decision making in special logic would be an "if-then-else" structure. For example, "if the proof is okay, then send it to the customer; else return to color correction."

Process logic lets us look at the larger picture. In this case, we would be interested to know exactly where "place hi-res files" fits within the overall production workflow. This is an important distinction, because we have two very different levels of workflow management to be concerned with: actions to perform specific tasks, and control and order of all tasks within the workflow.

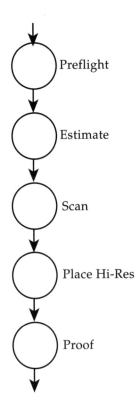

Tasks are used to organize the overall process logic.

How Deep Should You Look?
As you map out the workflow, it is important to find a balance between including enough tasks and procedures to give you a valuable picture of your workflow and including so many steps that the map becomes too cluttered to be useful. This is a very real danger because, as you will quickly begin to notice, these workflow charts can easily become so enormous that you can no longer clearly tell what is happening.

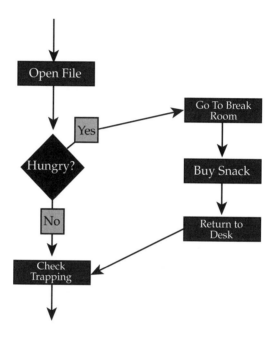

Inappropriate workflow maps only hinder the reengineering effort.

The best place to start mapping your workflow is at the highest levels. What is the overall flow of tasks through the system? Start by mapping some routine jobs through the plant, starting at preflight and working through platemaking. Compare the flow of good jobs (profitable ones) with the flow of bad jobs (unprofitable ones) through the shop. Because every company's workflow will be different, it is impossible to outline here all possible combinations. You must find out for yourself through this process what workflows exist in your shop.

After you do this for several jobs, you will notice that not all workflows are the same. Begin to think which people are involved within each workflow. In plants without stringent procedures in place, the workflow often will depend on who is involved, rather than what the best course of action should be. Some people will take advantage of new techniques, while others will be reticent to change methods that have worked for them for years. Look out for workflows that develop "personalities."

Once you have identified the participants in the workflow, you should begin thinking in terms of the skill sets required to produce the job. This will often identify areas where redundancy exists or where training could help streamline the workflow. Erase the names of people associated with each task and replace them with the skill set required to accomplish that task. This becomes a valuable tool for establishing training needs within the company.

After you have built some familiarity with mapping process logic through the plant, try breaking down a single task into its basic procedures. This moves us one level deeper into analyzing the workflow. Here is where you must be careful of overdoing it. We need to know what is involved in, for example, getting a color scan done, but we don't need to include what the operator had for lunch.

Mapping the set of procedures involved in a task lets us discover whether we are using all of our available resources and if there are redundant steps that could be eliminated. It also is the first stage in establishing useful sets of standard operating procedures for our employees. All too often, SOPs are written by a company officer with little knowledge of the day-to-day issues within a task or department. This can be an excellent opportunity for employee empowerment, allowing them the opportunity to use these tools as a method of self-improvement, while at the same time setting a benchmark standard for procedures within the company.

Mapping procedures also lets us clearly define responsibility for quality-control checks. Where exactly is work assessed in the workflow (or where should it be?), and who should perform the operation? Without a clear picture of your company's workflow, this very important job becomes a guessing game.

Other Mapping Strategies

The flow of work from task to task through a plant is not the only method available to us for assessing workflow. Remember that workflow is an all-inclusive process. We cannot look at only one aspect. Instead, we need to consider how we can map other influences on the workflow. One of the advantages realized as a result of workflow improvement is increased communications between participants and departments within the company. Often it can be helpful to map out the communications structure of the company. Who knows what is getting done within your company? What are their lines of communication, and how effective are those lines?

Often the CSR, who is responsible for communicating with the customer, is left completely out of the production loop. Likewise, scheduling needs to be informed of any unforeseen problems that occur with a job. Communication lines must be clear, and they must allow information to travel in both directions.

The physical layout of the shop is another area that may need to be mapped as a part of the workflow reengineering process. Work should move physically through the plant in a way that echoes the flow of the job from task to task. Is time being wasted while employees have to walk back and forth through the shop to reach essential equipment or supplies?

Though it may be impossible to completely restructure areas within the company where work gets done, relocating strategic equipment is often an accomplishable goal that will reduce the amount of time employees spend trudging around the company. Commonly used equipment like laser printers should be easily accessible to those who need it.

The time spent on particular tasks and procedures needs to be taken into account as well. This affects scheduling and is crucial in establishing accurate cost estimates for jobs. As you outline various workflows, try to track the times required to perform a task. Though all jobs will have varying levels of complexity, after several tries you should begin to see patterns developing. If tasks and procedures are consistently taking more time than expected to complete, you have begun to identify problem areas for cycle-time.

A final area to consider in workflow analysis is correction cycles. Who has the authority to initiate an internal rework, and what is that person's procedure for doing so? Building a map of these review cycles gives a graphical representation of the quality-control structure within the company and can help you to identify new locations to insert correction reviews.

It is especially important to take note of times when incorrect work falls through the cracks in a quality-control system and makes it out to the customer. By precisely mapping where the problem occurred, you can take appropriate action to prevent this error from happening again.

Conclusion

If you understand that workflow is a business problem and not a function of how much equipment you throw at it, you have taken the most important step toward increasing the efficiency and the profitability of your company. Technology in the graphic arts will continue to change and influence the way we do work. Making the proper use of new technology does not require a technological genius. It does require an understanding of the multiple parallel processes that influence the company.

The reason workflow has become so critical to profitability is that technology is essentially only as smart as the people who implement it. As you focus on process improvement, automation, and developing the skills of your employees, you will find that these critical areas have much more influence on your company's success than the type of equipment you choose to install.

Do not be frustrated if all your problems are not solved overnight. Successful workflow analysis and reengineering is a process best done slowly, and it's one that will never be completely finished. There will always be room for improvement within a company. Our permanent goal should be to find and exploit those opportunities.

Unlike other manufacturing assembly lines, graphic arts workflows do not follow a general model of the production process. Every printing plant is different. Every workflow is different. And every job is a surprise. With conventional workflow, the production process used to start with the printer or the prepress house. They received different kinds of artwork or raw text, and their job was to set type, scan images, build pages, make film and plates and finally print the job. They knew how to scan the images, whether transparencies or reflections, positives or negatives. They knew what colors were "reproducible," what the variability of the process was, and what file formats to use. The printer and/or the prepress service had almost everything under control.

Today we see the integration of the image creator with the production process itself. Most jobs today arrive in digital format. Designers as well as graphic artists are integrating computers into their work. Content creators are now doing some tasks that used to be done by printers or prepress houses, so printers and prepress services are losing control over file preparation for printing. And that file preparation controls the entire process.

Why Workflow Automation?

Automation permits the combination of complex and simple tasks that do not need manual intervention. The reasons we should do this are lower costs and faster deliveries. However, in graphic arts, there are probably as many exceptions as rules. Exceptions are those jobs that do not run easily through the workflow. Managing exceptions is more difficult. They are more expensive than managing regular standardized processes, because they require operator expertise and intervention.

This concept applies not only for the production process alone but also for customers, since they now have to archive, retrieve, manipulate, and reuse digital information. They must also deal with exceptions and lack of standardization.

Workflow Design

We can have as many workflow models as we wish. The bottom line is that when designing a workflow, it is necessary to analyze the different steps that are encountered most frequently. Then identify the individual processes to produce the desired results, and finally design a workflow, or a group of workflows, which can handle those steps in an efficient manner. The idea of workflow design is not to streamline each task in order to save time in each step of the process, but rather to automate the entire process. The whole is the sum of its parts.

File formats will come and go. Computers will become faster and faster. New processes for manufacturing work will be invented and implemented. But the basics of business—satisfying our customers—will always remain our primary challenge.

Glossary

Additive Color
A color space where other colors are derived by adding different amounts of red, green, and blue.

Addressability
The measure of total laser spots in a linear direction for an output device. Often called *resolution*.

ANSI (American National Standards Institute)
Organization responsible for administering industry standards within the United States.

APR (Automatic Picture Replacement)
A proprietary version of OPI used with Scitex equipment. *See also* OPI.

Bandwidth
A measure of networking speed capabilities, usually represented in megabits per second (Mbps).

Bit Depth
A representation of different tone values that can be represented by a single pixel. Bit depth is measured by exponential values of 2.

Bridge
Network hardware used to connect different network segments.

Calibration
The process of adjusting an output device to correct for inconsistencies in a printing system.

CCD (Charge-Coupled Device)
A type of sensor used in many desktop scanners and digital cameras to record images by converting light into electrical energy.

CD-R
A recordable version of compact disks.

CEPS (Color Electronic Prepress System)
Proprietary system for creating and editing color separations that preceded desktop computers.

CGATS (Committee for Graphic Arts Technology Standards)
Organization responsible for establishing standards in printing and publishing.

Characterization
The process of taking measurements from a test target to profile the exact inconsistencies inherent in a printing system.

CIE (International Commission on Illumination)
Organization responsible for recommending standards to ISO on illumination and color science.

CIE L*a*b* (CIELAB)
A three-dimensional device-independent color space used by color-management systems as an interim space for color transformations, and commonly used to represent color in colorimetry.

CIP3 (Consortium for Integrating Prepress, Press, and Postpress)
An organization working to create formats for digital files that can be generated in prepress and used to set up press and finishing devices.

Color-Management System (CMS)
A method of automating color control and reproduction by characterizing color systems and allowing a computer to make color transforms based on the resultant look-up tables.

Computer-to-Plate (CtP)
Generic description for workflow process where plates are directly imaged, rather than created through exposure to light.

CPU (Central Processing Unit)
Part of a computer that does processing, containing a main chip, memory, and connecting circuits.

CRT (Cathode Ray Tube)
A term for computer monitors, televisions, or other such devices that create images on a screen by exciting phosphors with an electron gun.

DCS (Desktop Color Separation)
A PostScript file format that is used with raster art to save specific color information into separate files.

Delta-E
A measure of the distance between two colors in CIELAB color space. The lower the number, the closer the colors; 0 represents a perfect match.

Densitometer
A device used to measure the absorption of light by a reflective or transmissive object, usually a photographic original, film, or press sheet.

Density
A logarithmic scale used to represent the absorption of light by an object. Higher values mean that more light is absorbed, thus the object appears darker.

Desktop Publishing (DTP)
Creating, editing, and processing digital documents using standard desktop computers and software.

Digital Press
A printing press that accepts digital files without any interim platemaking stage. Digital presses are characterized by reimaging an image carrier for each impression.

Direct Imaging Press
A traditional printing press that images plates directly on the press, then runs a number of static impressions.

Document Management
A strategy for controlling the creation and use of digital documents in a client/server environment.

Document Structuring Convention (DSC)
A manual released by Adobe Systems to provide some standardization to the PostScript page-description language. In theory, PostScript that is DSC compliant should image without problems on Adobe RIPs.

Dot Gain
A representation of a change in tone value as halftone dots increase in size due to the interaction of ink, press, and paper. Also called *tone value increase (TVI)*.

DVD
A recordable optical media that works similar to compact disks but can hold more information on a smaller format.

Dye Sublimation
A type of printer that works by using heat to transfer colorants from a donor sheet to paper.

EPS (Encapsulated PostScript)
A PostScript file format with an optional preview that can be placed into other applications.

Ethernet
A standard for network hardware common in the graphic arts.

GIF (Compuserve GIF)
A file format invented by Compuserve that uses indexed color space. GIF files are common on the Internet but inappropriate for high-end printing.

GRACoL (General Requirements and Applications
for Commercial Offset Lithography)
A set of standards designed to provide consistency in the design and processing of work for commercial offset printing.

Halftone
The result of dividing a continuous-tone original into small dots of varying sizes so the image can be reproduced on a printing press.

Hub
Network hardware that allows multiple workstations to connect to a central location.

ICC (International Color Consortium)
Organization, comprising graphic arts–related companies, that establishes standards for color management systems.

Imagesetter
A device that is used to digitally expose film for printing processes.

Indexed Color
A color space that limits the total number of colors used in a file, usually 8-bit or 256 colors.

Inkjet
A type of printer that works by placing drops of aqueous dyes onto paper.

Interpolation
A process where pixels and image data are artificially created by a computer based on estimates of surrounding tone or pixel values.

ISO (International Standards Organization)
Body responsible for establishing international industry standards.

JAZ
A type of popular removable media from Iomega.

JPEG (Joint Photographic Experts Group)
A file format using lossy compression. Commonly used for images on the Internet but inappropriate for use in high-end printing.

L*a*b*
See CIE L*a*b*

Linearization
The process of optimizing an output device so that input values match output values.

Line Art
A type of artwork with a bit depth of 1.

LocalTalk
Low-bandwidth networking protocol that is built into Apple Macintosh computers.

Magneto Optical Disks (MO)
A type of removable media that achieved limited success in the United States but is still in widespread use in other countries.

NORM (Normalize Once—Rasterize Many)
A workflow process where files are interpreted once and then sent to multiple output devices.

Operating System
Primary software on a computer that allows other applications to interact with the device's hardware. Windows, Macintosh, and UNIX are three common operating systems.

OPI (Open Prepress Interface)
A system invented by Aldus in which low-resolution image files placed into a layout are replaced with high-resolution equivalents when printed.

PDF (Portable Document Format)
A file format, created by Adobe Systems, used as an intermediary for transporting files from creator to manufacturer.

Peripheral
Generic term for any external device connected to a computer.

Pixel
A pixel (from "picture element") is the smallest component of a piece of raster art.

Platesetter
A device used to digitally expose plates for printing processes. Also known as *CTP* or *computer-to-plate*. Plates can be made for flexography, gravure, and offset lithography from digital data, on metal or polyester plates.

PMT (Photomultiplier Tube)
A very sensitive device used by high-end and mid-range drum scanners to record images by converting light into electrical energy.

PostScript
A page-description language developed by Adobe Systems in 1985. It is the language understood by virtually all printers in the graphic arts.

Preflight
Graphics arts term that represents the process of checking incoming files to ensure that they conform with workflow requirements.

Print Server
A special type of server that can queue, route, and control printer jobs.

RAM (Random-Access Memory)
Part of a computer that temporarily stores software and files while they are actively being used by the system.

Raster Art
A type of digital artwork composed of a grid of pixels. Raster art is usually used for photographs.

Repeatability
A measure of how closely a printing process can create equal reproductions from impression to impression.

RIP (Raster Image Processor)
Interpreter connected to a printer that translates incoming printer files, usually in PostScript, into a format that can be imaged by a marking engine.

ROOM (RIP Once—Output Many)
A workflow process in which files are interpreted once and then sent to multiple output devices.

Router
Network hardware that connects segments as well as directing information to specific workstations.

SCSI (Small Computer Systems Interface)
Connectivity standard for attaching peripherals to a computer that is common in the graphic arts. Pronounced "scuzzy."

SNAP (Specifications for Non-Heatset Advertising Printing)
A set of standards designed to provide consistency in the design and processing of advertising work for newspaper printing.

Sneakernet
A slang term for using removable media instead of networks to move files from computer to computer.

Spectrophotometer
A device used to measure the color of an object by calculating reflectance across the entire visual spectrum.

Spot
A unit measure (also called *element* and *machine dot*) that refers to the diameter of exposure on film, paper, or plates from a single modulation of the laser. Halftone dots are created from multiple laser spots.

SWOP (Specifications for Web Offset Publications)
A set of standards designed to provide consistency in the design and processing of advertising work for web offset printing.

TCP/IP
A telecommunications protocol used for the Internet and for some networking systems.

Thermal Imaging
Refers to directly imaging printing plates coated with a heat-

reactive photopolymer by exposing them with a laser operating at 830nm or higher.

Tone Value Increase (TVI)
See Dot Gain

Trapping
1) In process control, a densitometric derived value for how well one ink transfers to another ink. 2) In prepress, the creation of slight overlaps between colors (spreads and chokes) that corrects for inherent registration errors on presses.

Server
Central computer that serves as a central storage location for files and/or programs on a network.

Status A
A standard that defines how densitometers should be set up to take measurements. Status A is used in Europe.

Status T
A standard that defines how densitometers should be set up to take measurements. Status T is used in the United States.

Subtractive Color
A color space where other colors are derived by subtracting specific wavelengths from light by absorption from cyan, magenta, and yellow colorants.

TIFF (Tagged Image File Format)
A standard file format commonly used to save raster art used in high-end printing.

TIFF /IT
An intermediary file format used to transport files from creator to manufacturer.

UNIX
A reliable operating system commonly used for large mainframe computers or network servers.

USB (Universal Serial Bus)
Relatively new connectivity standard for desktop computers that allows more functionality than SCSI.

Vector Art
A type of digital artwork where the elements are represented using mathematical curves. Vector art is usually used for illustrations.

Volatile Memory
See RAM

Workflow Server
A special type of server that can control print jobs, as well as perform other tasks like trapping or color separations.

ZIP
1) A type of popular removable media from Iomega. 2) A lossless compression algorithm used primarily with the Windows operating system.

Index

A
Additive color, 119, 225
Addressability, 129, 132, 225
Adobe Acrobat, 92, 124, 178
Adobe Distiller, 92, 198, 199
Adobe Systems, 4, 17, 31, 79, 82, 89, 90, 92, 120, 228, 230, 231
Aldus, 4, 15, 85, 230
American National Standards Institute, 31, 32, 225
ANSI, *see* American National Standards Institute
APR, 56, 225
ASCII, 79, 80, 90

B
Bandwidth, 48, 93, 225, 230
Bit depth, 80, 82, 83, 84, 99, 225, 230
Blueline, 113, 114, 115
Bridge, 50, 51, 225

C
Calibration, 7, 23, 113, 117, 121, 122, 147, 193, 225
Canon, 117
Capstan imagesetter, 16, 139, 140
Cathode ray tube (CRT), 13, 119, 120, 227
CCD, *see* Charge-coupled device
CD-R, 70, 71, 74, 75, 166, 226
CD-ROM, 42, 69, 70
CEPS, *see* Color Electronic Prepress System
CGATS, *see* Committee for Graphic Arts Technology Standards
Characterization, 33, 190, 226
Charge-coupled device, 99, 103, 226
CIE, 32, 226
CIE L*a*b*, 105, 106, 226, 227

CIP3, 156, 226
Client/server, 54, 228
Color Electronic Prepress System, 15, 17, 31, 97, 226
Color management, 33, 44, 105, 106, 107, 108, 110, 117, 118, 192, 193, 194, 195, 203, 229
Color-rendering dictionaries, 194
ColorArt, 115
ColorSync, 107, 198
Committee for Graphic Arts Technology Standards, 9, 32, 92, 120, 178, 226
Compuserve, 94, 228
Computer-to-plate, 8, 18, 29, 21, 24, 26, 27, 28, 100, 111, 112, 113, 141, 147, 160, 163, 226, 231
Consortium for the Integration of Prepress, Press, and Postpress, 156, 226
Copy-dot scanner, 100, 160
CPU, 37, 38, 39, 40, 41, 65, 227
CRD, 194
Creo Spectrum, 118
CRT, 13, 119, 120, 226
CSR (customer service representative), 158, 211, 212, 219
CTP, *see* computer-to-plate

D
DAT, 62, 70, 71, 74, 75
DCS, 85, 86, 227
Delta-E, 227
Densitometer, 9 23, 30, 100, 227, 233
Density, 22, 98, 116, 227
Desktop publishing, 6, 15, 16, 17, 22, 24, 30, 36, 44, 66, 67, 70, 97, 139, 227
Digital press, 6, 19, 22, 117, 133, 134, 135, 136, 147, 148, 151, 165, 227
Digital printing, 6, 19, 20, 24, 100, 110
Digital proofs, 35, 58, 107, 108, 114, 115, 116, 117, 118, 120, 122, 164, 194
Direct imaging press, 19, 20, 24, 147, 227
Direct-to-press, 19, 165, 176
Distribute and print, 6
Document management, 149, 151, 153, 195, 210, 228
Document Structuring Conventions (DSC), 31, 228
Dot gain, 23, 33, 35, 100, 101, 116, 122, 145, 147, 192, 228
Drum imagesetter, 16, 139, 140
Drum platesetter, 18, 142, 143

DVD, 71, 74, 75, 166, 228
Dye sublimation, 117, 228
Dylux, 113, 114

E
Encapsulated PostScript, *see* EPS
EPS, 85, 887, 89, 228
Epson 5000, 120
Ethernet, 15, 46, 47, 49, 50, 52, 72, 228

F
Floppy disks, 14, 40, 66, 67, 70
FM screening, 122
Fuji, 103, 104, 115

G
GCR, 101, 107
GIF, 94, 228
Gigabit Ethernet, 49
GRACoL, 9, 36, 102, 228

H
Halftone, 26, 81, 84, 100, 115, 118, 119, 129, 131, 228, 229, 232
Harlequin, 45
Heidelberg, 20, 45, 205
        Delta, 45
        Quickmaster DI, 19
Hewlett-Packard, 124
Hot folders, 191, 199, 200, 201, 202
Hub, 43, 50, 229

I
ICC, *see* International Color Consortium
Imagesetters, 15, 16, 17, 18, 23, 24, 58, 81, 83, 86, 89, 123, 124, 125,
        126, 128, 129, 133, 135, 139, 140, 141, 142, 143, 229
Imation, 115
Imposition, 18, 60, 73, 74, 90, 107, 113, 141, 152, 157, 162, 163, 164,
        165, 171, 174, 175, 176, 185, 190, 191, 192, 200, 201, 202, 211, 212,
        214
In-RIP trapping, 211
Indexed color, 94, 228, 229
Indigo, 117
Inkjet, 105, 118, 119, 120, 135, 137, 138, 139, 229
International Color Consortium, 9, 32, 33, 105, 107, 108, 110, 116,

120, 194, 229
International Standards Organization, 9, 24, 32, 226, 227, 229
Internet, 14, 21, 25, 50, 54, 62, 63, 64, 75, 92, 94, 110, 121, 133, 134,
   135, 150, 196, 228, 229, 232
Interpolation, 98, 229
Iomega, 70
         JAZ, 69, 229
         ZIP, 68, 234
IRIS, 118, 120
ISDN, 120
ISO, *see* International Standards Organization
ISO 9000, 26

J
Job tickets, 152–153, 176, 177, 178
Job tracking, 152–153
JPEG, 94, 229

K
Kodak Approval, 118

L
L*a*b*, *see* CIE L*a*b*
Line art, 83, 84, 85, 160, 230
Linearization, 23, 230
Linotronic, 16
Linotype, 4, 16
LocalTalk, 48, 228

M
Macintosh, 4, 14, 15, 37, 38, 39, 41, 42, 43, 45, 46, 48, 49, 55, 57, 69,
   92, 107, 111, 123, 198, 230
Mac OS, 13, 43, 46
         Servers, 54
Magneto optical disks, 68, 230
Mainframe, 11, 13, 45, 65, 233
MatchPrint, 115
Microsoft Internet Explorer, 94
Microsoft Windows, 13, 38, 42, 43, 44, 45, 46, 55, 67, 92, 107, 123,
   230, 234
Microsoft Windows NT, 45, 55
Multimedia, 21, 25, 93, 110, 133, 135, 152

N

Netscape Navigator, 94
Network, 14, 25, 43, 45, 46, 47–52, 53, 54, 55, 56, 57, 58, 62, 63, 71,
      73, 93, 94, 108, 109, 120, 121, 124, 132, 134, 151, 156, 160, 162, 163,
      166, 167, 179, 195, 199, 201, 206, 224, 225, 228, 229, 230, 232, 233
Normalize Once—Rasterize Many (NORM), 126, 132, 133, 188,
      230

O
Open Prepress Interface, *see* OPI
Operating system, 13, 33, 37, 40, 43, 44, 45, 54, 55, 106, 167, 196,
      198, 230, 232, 234
OPI, 56, 57, 58, 60, 73, 86, 108, 109, 162, 224, 230

P
PageMaker, 4, 14, 17, 89, 106
PCL, 124
PDF, 89, 90, 92, 93, 120, 124, 126, 132, 178, 199, 230
PDF/X, 92, 120, 178
Peripheral, 42, 230
Photomultiplier tube, 15, 99, 103, 230
PIA, 35, 183
PIA Ratios, 183
Pixel, 41, 80, 81, 82, 83, 84, 88, 93, 98, 99, 128, 131, 132, 225, 229,
      230, 231
Platesetter, 18, 19, 135, 141, 142, 143, 146, 164, 165, 231
PMT, *see* Photomultiplier tube
Polaroid PolaProof, 118
Portable Document Format, *see* PDF
PostScript, 4, 14, 15, 16, 17, 18, 30, 44, 46, 73, 78, 79, 85, 86, 88, 89,
      90, 92, 93, 108, 110, 111, 122, 124, 125, 126, 161, 165, 199, 212, 227,
      228, 229, 231
PostScript 3, 129
Preflighting, 37, 152, 159, 160, 161, 162, 170, 178, 181, 183, 185, 190,
      192, 197, 198, 205, 208, 212, 214, 217, 230
Presstek, 118
Printing Industries of America, 35, 183
Proofing, 7, 22, 23, 35, 60, 76, 89, 90, 108, 111–122, 123, 132, 137,
      161, 164, 165, 170, 172, 174, 179, 181, 190, 192, 194, 197, 202

Q
Quark, 17
QuarkXPress, 17, 89, 107, 174

R

RAID, 62
RAM (random-access memory), 37, 39–40, 41, 46, 231
Raster art, 80, 231
Raster image processor, 15, 16, 17, 19, 23, 45, 54, 62, 81, 83, 86, 88,
    89, 90, 92, 108, 110, 123, 124, 125, 126, 128, 131, 132, 133, 134,
    155, 156, 163, 165, 171, 174, 176, 188, 194, 198, 199, 209, 211, 226,
    230, 231
Repeatability, 22, 231
RIP, *see* Raster image processor
RIP Once—Output Many (ROOM), 126, 132, 133, 188, 232
Router, 50, 51, 232

S
Scitex, 15, 31, 45, 55, 56, 93, 118, 225
        APR, 56
        CT, 31
Scripts, 150, 176, 191, 197, 198, 199, 201
SCSI, 42, 43, 69, 232, 234
Server, 45, 47, 53–64, 92, 134, 150, 152, 153, 162, 166, 176, 194, 195,
    196, 214, 233
        Applications server, 54, 60
        File server, 53, 56, 58, 60, 72
        Print server, 53, 58, 60, 174, 229, 231
        Security, 62–64
        Workflow server, 53, 60, 72, 134, 174, 176, 234
Small Computer Systems Interface, *see* SCSI
SNAP, 9, 35, 36, 102, 232
Sneakernet, 71, 72, 232
Soft proofing, 7, 111, 119, 120, 164
Spectrophotometer, 9, 23, 193, 232
Spot, 128, 141, 144, 232
Status A, 30, 233
Status T, 30, 233
Subtractive color, 119, 233
SWOP, 9, 34–35, 36, 102, 232
SyQuest, 67, 68, 69, 70, 75

T
TAC, *see* Total area coverage
TCP/IP (Telecommunications Protocol/Internet Protocol), 14, 50
Thermal imaging, 19, 143, 232
Thermal wax, 117
TIFF, 85, 92, 199, 233

TIFF/IT, 90, 92–93, 233
Tone value increase, 228
Total area coverage, 101–102, 107
Trapping, 60, 93, 113, 133, 134, 163, 165, 174, 202, 210, 214, 233, 234

U
UCR, 101, 107
Universal Serial Bus, *see* USB
UNIX, 43, 45, 55, 92, 123, 230, 233
USA Today, 29, 35
USB, 42, 43, 232

V
Variable-data printing, 6, 19, 148
Vector art, 86, 88, 89, 232
Volatile memory, 13, 39, 234
VRAM, 37, 41, 42, 46

W
WHAM!NET, 75, 121
Winchester disk drive, 14
Windows, *see* Microsoft Windows

X
Xeikon, 19, 117
Xerox, 13, 15, 117
      Palo Alto Research Center, 13, 49
      DocuColor 40, 19

About the Author

Ric Withers is Director of Imaging Technologies for IO Technologies and has more than ten years experience working in computers, commercial lithography, digital printing, and Internet publishing. He holds a Master of Science degree in Graphic Arts Systems from the Rochester Institute of Technology, where he specialized in color proofing and workflow systems. Ric lives in Richmond, Virginia, and can be contacted at rwiths@aol.com.

Illustrations by Amy Ketterer